Andrew Mckie, Barrister at Clerksroom Manchester, is a specialist in claimant and defendant personal injury, travel and housing law practitioner. Andrew is also now co-owner of a Law Firm in Manchester, Barrister-Direct Limited, where he practices in personal injury, travel and housing law including housing disrepair and cavity wall claims.

Ian Skeate, Barrister joined Clerksroom in January 2010 after practising from St Johns Buildings, Manchester since 2003. He has particular expertise in Personal Injury, Professional Discipline and Regulation, Employment and Costs. Ian is based in Manchester but his practice extends throughout the country especially in London.

A Practical Guide to Industrial Disease Claims

A Practical Guide to Industrial Disease Claims

Andrew Mckie,
Barrister at Law, Clerksroom (Manchester),
LLB Hons, PG DIP and
Former Solicitor Advocate,
Personal Injury, Fraud, Credit Hire

Ian Skeate, Barrister at Law, Clerksroom (Manchester),
BA/MA (Cantab), Personal Injury, Costs,
Disciplinary/Regulatory Work

Law Brief Publishing

Published 2018 by Law Brief Publishing, an imprint of Law Brief Publishing Ltd
30 The Parks
Minehead
Somerset
TA24 8BT

www.lawbriefpublishing.com

Paperback: 978-1-911035-83-1

PREFACE

The upcoming changes to the Small Claims Track in personal injury are likely to come into effect in October 2019. This book looks at industrial disease claims.

This book covers matters of industrial disease, and in particular focuses on the day-to-day issues in practice that one encounters with such cases including spotting the 'winners' and 'losers' quickly, practical tips for investigation, litigation tactics, as well as a summary of the law, the important cases, and how to run these claims efficiently.

In addition to general handling, the chapters in this book cover the nature of the claim and technical background, relevant standards, who to sue, allegations of negligence and breach of duty, disclosure, remedies, expert evidence, causation, quantum and costs.

This is a book that any personal injury practitioner, looking to diversify into these areas, should not be without.

The law is accurate as at 12th October 2018.

Andrew Mckie
Ian Skeate
October 2018

CONTENTS

CHAPTER ONE

AN INTRODUCTION TO INDUSTRIAL DISEASE CLAIMS – GENERAL PRINCIPLES INCLUDING LIMITATION, BREACH OF DUTY AND EXPERT EVIDENCE

LEGAL PRINCIPLES

To found a claim in negligence and/or breach of statutory duty, the claimant has to prove:

1. His condition was caused by occupational exposure in breach of duty;
2. He is within the limitation period;
3. A defendant can be readily identified who is worth suing, i.e., solvent and/or insured even if they are no longer operating or on the register of companies.

The Pre-Action Protocol for Disease and Illness Claims should be followed and full disclosure obtained, as soon as possible. The Protocol sets out:-

1 INTRODUCTION

1.1

Lord Woolf in his final Access to Justice Report of July 1996 recommended the development of protocols: 'To build on and increase the benefits of early but well informed settlements which genuinely satisfy both parties to a dispute.'

1.2

The aims of these protocols are:

. more contact between the parties
. better and earlier exchange of information
. better investigation by both sides
. to put the parties in a position where they may be able to settle cases fairly and early without litigation
. to enable proceedings to run to the court's timetable and efficiently, if litigation does become necessary.

1.3

The concept of protocols is relevant to a range of initiatives for good claims practice, especially:

. predictability in the time needed for steps to be taken
. standardisation of relevant information, including documents to be disclosed.

1.4

The Courts will be able to treat the standards set in protocols as the normal reasonable approach. If proceedings are issued, it will be for the court to decide whether non-compliance with a protocol should merit adverse consequences. Guidance on the court's likely approach will be given from time to time in practice directions.

1.5

If the court has to consider the question of compliance after proceedings have begun, it will not be concerned with minor infringements, e.g. failure by a short period to provide relevant information. One minor breach will not exempt the 'innocent' party from following the protocol. The court will look at the effect of non-compliance on the other party when deciding whether to impose sanctions.

2 NOTES OF GUIDANCE - SCOPE OF THE PROTOCOL

2.1

This protocol is intended to apply to all personal injury claims where the injury is not as the result of an accident but takes the form of an illness or disease.

2.2

This protocol covers disease claims which are likely to be complex and frequently not suitable for fast-track procedures even though they may fall within fast track limits. Disease for the purpose of this protocol primarily covers any illness physical or psychological, any disorder, ailment, affliction, complaint, malady, or derangement other than a physical or psychological injury solely caused by an accident or other similar single event.

2.3

In appropriate cases it may be agreed between the parties that this protocol can be applied rather than the Pre-Action Protocol for Personal Injury Claims where a single event occurs but causes a disease or illness.

2.4

This protocol is not limited to diseases occurring in the workplace but will embrace diseases occurring in other situations for example through occupation of premises or the use of products. It is not intended to cover those cases, which are dealt with as a 'group' or 'class' action.

2.5

The 'cards on the table' approach advocated by the Pre-Action Protocol for Personal Injury Claims is equally appropriate to disease claims. The spirit of that protocol, and of the clinical negligence pro-

tocol is followed here, in accordance with the sense of the civil justice reforms.

2.6

The timetable and the arrangements for disclosing documents and obtaining expert evidence may need to be varied to suit the circumstances of the case. If a party considers the detail of the protocol to be inappropriate they should communicate their reasons to all of the parties at that stage. If proceedings are subsequently issued, the court will expect an explanation as to why the protocol has not been followed, or has been varied.

2.7

In a terminal disease claim with short life expectancy, for instance where a claimant has a disease such as mesothelioma, the time scale of the protocol is likely to be too long. In such a claim, the claimant may not be able to follow the protocol and the defendant would be expected to treat the claim with urgency including any request for an interim payment.

2.8

In a claim for mesothelioma, additional provisions apply, which are set out in Annex C of this protocol.

2A ALTERNATIVE DISPUTE RESOLUTION

2A.1

The parties should consider whether some form of alternative dispute resolution procedure would be more suitable than litigation, and if so, endeavour to agree which form to adopt. Both the Claimant and Defendant may be required by the Court to provide evidence that alternative means of resolving their dispute were considered. The Courts take the view that litigation should be a last resort, and that claims should not be issued prematurely when a settlement is still actively being explored. Parties are warned that if the protocol is not followed (including this paragraph) then the Court must have regard to such conduct when determining costs.

2A.2

It is not practicable in this protocol to address in detail how the parties might decide which method to adopt to resolve their particular dispute. However, summarised below are some of the options for resolving disputes without litigation:

. Discussion and negotiation.
. Early neutral evaluation by an independent third party (for example, a lawyer experienced in the field of disease or illness, or an individual experienced in the subject matter of the claim).
. Mediation – a form of facilitated negotiation assisted by an independent neutral party,
. Arbitration (where an independent person or body makes a binding decision).
2A.3

The Legal Services Commission has published a booklet on 'Alternatives to Court', CLS Direct Information Leaflet 23 (http://www.communitylegaladvice.org.uk/media/808/FD/leaflet23e.pdf), which lists a number of organisations that provide alternative dispute resolution services.

2A.4

It is expressly recognised that no party can or should be forced to mediate or enter into any form of ADR, but the parties should continue to consider the possibility of reaching a settlement at all times.

3 THE AIMS OF THE PROTOCOL

3.1

The general aims of the protocol are –

. to resolve as many disputes as possible without litigation;
. where a claim cannot be resolved to identify the relevant issues which remain in dispute.

3.2

The specific objectives are –

OPENNESS

. to encourage early communication of the perceived problem between the parties or their insurers;
. to encourage employees to voice any concerns or worries about possible work related illness as soon as practicable;
. to encourage employers to develop systems of early reporting and investigation of suspected occupational health problems and to provide full and prompt explanations to concerned employees or former employees;
. to apply such principles to perceived problems outside the employer/employee relationship, for example occupiers of premises or land and producers of products;
. to ensure that sufficient information is disclosed by both parties to enable each to understand the other's perspective and case, and to encourage early resolution;

TIMELINESS

. to provide an early opportunity for employers (past or present) or their insurers to identify cases where an investigation is required and to carry out that investigation promptly;
. to encourage employers (past or present) or other defendants to involve and identify their insurers at an early stage;
. to ensure that all relevant records including health and personnel records are provided to employees (past or present) or their appointed representatives promptly on request, by any employer (past or present) or their insurers. This should be complied with to a realistic timetable;

. to ensure that relevant records which are in the claimant's possession including where appropriate GP and hospital records are made available to the defendant or to the nominated insurance manager or solicitor representing the defendant by claimants or their advisers at an appropriate stage;

. to proceed on a reasonable timetable where a resolution is not achievable to lay the ground to enable litigation to proceed at a reasonable and proportionate cost, and to limit the matters in contention;

. to communicate promptly where any of the requested information is not available or does not exist;

. to discourage the prolonged pursuit of unmeritorious claims and the prolonged defence of meritorious claims;

. to encourage all parties, at the earliest possible stage, to disclose voluntarily any additional documents which will assist in resolving any issue;

. to promote the provision of medical or rehabilitation treatment in appropriate cases to address the needs of the claimant.

4 THE PROTOCOL

This protocol is not a comprehensive code governing all the steps in disease claims. Rather it attempts to set out ***a code of good practice*** *which parties should follow.*

This protocol must be read in conjunction with the Practice Direction on Pre-Action Conduct.

OBTAINING OCCUPATIONAL RECORDS INCLUDING HEALTH RECORDS

4.1

In appropriate cases, a potential claimant may request Occupational Records including Health Records and Personnel Records before sending a Letter of Claim.

4.2

Any request for records by the potential claimant or his adviser should provide sufficient information to alert the potential defendant or his insurer where a possible disease claim is being investigated; Annex A1 provides a suggested form for this purpose for use in cases arising from employment. *Similar forms can be prepared and used in other situations.*

4.3

The copy records should be provided ***within a maximum of 40 days*** *of the request at no cost. Although these will primarily be occupational records, it will be good practice for a* ***potential defendant*** *to disclose product data documents identified by a* ***potential claimant*** *at this stage which may resolve a causation issue.*

4.4

Where the ***potential defendant*** *or his insurer has difficulty in providing information quickly (in particular where the information is, or may be, held by someone else such as the Health and Safety Executive) details should be provided of steps being taken to resolve this problem together with a reasonable time estimate for doing so.*

4.5

If the ***potential defendant*** *or his insurer fails to provide the records including health records within 40 days and fails to comply with paragraph 4.4 above, the* ***potential claimant*** *or his adviser may then apply to the court for an* ***order for pre-action disclosure****. The Civil Procedure Rules make pre-action applications to the court easier. The court also has the power to impose costs sanctions for unreasonable delay in providing records.*

5 COMMUNICATION

5.1

If either the ***potential claimant*** *or his adviser considers* ***additional records are required from a third party****, such as records from previous employers or GP and hospital records, in the first instance these should be requested by the* ***potential claimant*** *or their advisers. Third party record holders would be expected to co-operate. The Civil Procedure Rules enable parties to apply to the court for pre-action disclosure by third parties.*

5.2

As soon as the records have been received and analysed, the ***potential claimant*** *or his adviser should consider whether a claim should be made. GP and hospital records will normally be obtained before a decision is reached.*

5.3

If a decision is made not to proceed further at this stage against a party identified as a ***potential defendant****, the* ***potential claimant*** *or his adviser should notify that* ***potential defendant*** *in writing as soon as practicable.*

6 LETTER OF CLAIM

6.1

Where a decision is made to make a claim, the claimant shall send to the proposed defendant two copies of a letter of claim, as soon as sufficient information is available to substantiate a realistic claim and before issues of quantum are addressed in detail. One copy is for the defendants, the second for passing on to his insurers.

6.2

This letter shall contain a ***clear summary of the facts*** *on which the claim is based, including details of the illness or disease alleged, and the* ***main allegations of fault****. It shall also give details of present condition and prognosis. The* ***financial loss*** *incurred by the claimant should be outlined. Where the case is funded by a conditional fee agreement, notification should be given of the existence of the agreement and where appropriate, that there is a success fee and insurance premium, although not the level of the success fee or premium.*

6.3

Where the funding arrangement is an insurance policy the party must state –

(1) the name and address of the insurer;

(2) the policy number;

(3) the date of the policy;

(4) the claim or claims to which it relates (including Part 20 claims if any);

(5) the level of cover; and

(6) whether the premiums are staged and if so the points at which the increased premiums are payable.

6.4

Solicitors are recommended to use ***a standard format*** *for such a letter – an example is at Annex B: this can be amended to suit the particular case, for example, if the client has rehabilitation needs these can also be detailed in the letter.*

6.5

*A **chronology** of the relevant events (e.g. dates or periods of exposure) should be provided. **In the case of alleged occupational disease an appropriate employment history should also be provided (with a work history from HM Revenue and Customs),** particularly if the claimant has been employed by a number of different employers and the illness in question has a long latency period. Where there is more than one employer the chronology should state if there was any relevant exposure during each of those different periods of employment. **Details should also be given about any periods of self-employment during which there was any relevant exposure** and whether any claims have been made and payments received under the Pneumoconiosis etc. (Workers' Compensation) Act 1979.*

6.6

*The letter of claim should identify any **relevant documents,** including health records not already in the defendant's possession e.g. any relevant GP and hospital records. These will need to be disclosed in confidence to the nominated insurance manager or solicitor representing the defendant following receipt of their letter of acknowledgement. Where the action is brought under the Law Reform Act 1934 or the Fatal Accidents Act 1976 then **relevant documents** will normally include copies of the death certificate, the post mortem report, the inquest depositions and if obtained by that date the grant of probate or letters of administration.*

6.7

*The letter of claim should indicate whether a claim is also being made against any **other potential defendant** and identify any known insurer involved. **Copies of any relevant result from the Association of British Insurers Employers' Liability Tracing Service, both positive and negative, should be attached to the letter of claim**. If the claimant receives any insurance database results after sending the letter of claim those results should be forwarded to the defendant as soon as is reasonably practicable.*

6.8

Sufficient information should be given to enable the defendant's insurer/solicitor to commence ***investigations*** *and at least to put a broad valuation on the 'risk'.*

6.9

It is not a requirement for the claimant to provide ***medical evidence*** *with the letter of claim, but the claimant may choose to do so in very many cases.*

6.10

Letters of claim and response *are not intended to have the same* ***status*** *as a statement of case in proceedings. Matters may come to light as a result of investigation after the letter of claim has been sent, or after the defendant has responded, particularly if disclosure of documents takes place outside the recommended 90 day period. These circumstances could mean that the 'pleaded' case of one or both parties is presented slightly differently than in the letter of claim or response. It would not be consistent with the spirit of the protocol for a party to 'take a point' on this in the proceedings, provided that there was no obvious intention by the party who changed their position to mislead the other party.*

6.10A

Where a claim no longer continues under the Pre-Action Protocol for Low Value Personal Injury (Employers' Liability and Public Liability) Claims, the Claim Notification Form ('CNF') completed by the claimant under that Protocol can be used as the letter of claim under this protocol unless the defendant has notified the claimant that there is inadequate information in the CNF.

6.11

Proceedings should not be issued until after 90 days from the date of acknowledgement *(see paragraph 7), unless there is a limitation problem and/or the claimant's position needs to be protected by early issue. (See paragraphs 2.6 and 2.7)*

7 THE RESPONSE

7.1

The defendant should ***send an acknowledgement within 21 days*** *of the date of posting of the letter of claim, identifying the liability insurer (if any) who will be dealing with the matter and, if necessary, identifying specifically any significant omissions from the Letter of Claim. If there has been no acknowledgement by the defendant or insurer within 21 days, the claimant will be entitled to issue proceedings.*

7.2

The identity of all relevant insurers, if more than one, should be notified to the claimant by the insurer identified in the acknowledgement letter, within 30 days of the date of that acknowledgement. *For claims with a long latency period it is recognised that it may not be possible to identify the full insurance history within 30 days. In these circumstances the insurer or defendant should notify the claimant in writing as soon as possible. In any event, within 30 days the insurer or the defendant should state which other insurers have been identified. Where insurers have not been identified the defendant or insurer should state what steps have been taken to determine this information.*

7.3

The defendant or his representative should, ***within 90 days of the date of the acknowledgement letter****, provide a* ***reasoned answer:*** *–*

- *if the* ***claim is admitted****, they should say so in clear terms;*
- *if only* ***part of the claim is admitted*** *they should make clear which issues of fault and/or causation and/or limitation are admitted and which remain in issue and why;*
- *if the* ***claim is not admitted in full****, they should explain why and should,* ***for example****, include comments on the employment status of the claimant, (including job description(s) and details of the department(s) where the claimant worked), the allegations of fault, causation and of limitation, and if a synopsis or chronology of relevant events has been provided and is disputed, their version of those events;*
- *if the* ***claim is not admitted in full****, the defendant should enclose with his letter of reply* ***documents*** *in his possession which are* ***material to the issues*** *between the parties and which would be likely to be ordered to be disclosed by the court, either on an application for pre-action disclosure, or on disclosure during proceedings. Reference can be made to the documents annexed to the personal injury protocol.*
- *where more than one defendant receives a letter of claim, the timetable will be activated for each defendant by the date on the letter of claim addressed to them. If any defendant wishes to extend the timetable because the number of defendants will cause complications, they should seek agreement to a different timetable as soon as possible.*

7.4

If the parties reach agreement on liability and/or causation, but time is needed to resolve other issues including the value of the claim, they should aim to agree a reasonable period.

7.5

Where it is not practicable for the defendant to complete his investigations within 90 days, the defendant should indicate the difficulties and outline the further time needed. Any request for an extension of time should be made, with reasons, as soon as the defendant becomes aware that an extension is needed and normally before the 90 day period has expired. Such an extension of time should be agreed in circumstances where reasonable justification has been shown. Lapse of many years since the circumstances giving rise to the claim does not, by itself, constitute reasonable justification for further time.

7.6

Where the relevant negligence occurred outside England and Wales and/or where the defendant is outside the jurisdiction, the time periods of 21 days and 90 days should normally be extended up to 42 days and 180 days.

8 SPECIAL DAMAGES

8.1

The claimant will send to the defendant as soon as practicable a Schedule of Special Damages with supporting documents, particularly where the defendant has admitted liability.

9 EXPERTS

9.1

In disease claims expert opinions may be needed on one or more of the following –

- ***knowledge, fault, causation and apportionment;***
- ***condition and prognosis;***
- ***valuing aspects of the claim.***

9.2

The civil justice reforms and the Civil Procedure Rules encourage economy in the use of experts and a less adversarial expert culture. It is recognised that in disease claims, the parties and their advisers will require flexibility in their approach to expert evidence. Decisions on whether experts might be instructed jointly, and on whether reports might be disclosed sequentially or by exchange, should rest with the parties and their advisers. Sharing expert evidence may be appropriate on various issues including those relating to the value of the claim. However, this protocol does not attempt to be prescriptive on issues in relation to expert evidence.

9.3

Obtaining expert evidence will often be an expensive step and may take time, especially in specialised areas where there are limited numbers of suitable experts. Claimants, defendants and their advisers, will therefore need to consider carefully how best to obtain any necessary expert help quickly and cost-effectively.

9.4

The protocol recognises that a flexible approach must be adopted in the obtaining of medical reports in claims of this type. There will be very many occasions where the claimant will need to obtain a medical report before writing the letter of claim. In such cases the defendant will be entitled to obtain their own medical report. In some other instances it may be more appropriate to send the letter of claim before the medical report is obtained. Defendants will usually need to see a medical report before they can reach a view on causation.

9.5

Where the parties agree the nomination of a single expert is appropriate, before any party instructs an expert he should give the other party a list of the ***name(s)*** *of* ***one or more experts*** *in the relevant speciality whom he considers are suitable to instruct. The parties are encouraged to agree the instruction of a single expert to deal with discrete areas such as cost of care.*

9.6

Within 14 days *the other party may indicate* ***an objection*** *to one or more of the named experts. The first party should then instruct a mutually acceptable expert. If the Claimant nominates an expert in the original letter of claim, the 14 days is in addition to the 21 days in paragraph 7.1.*

9.7

If the second party objects to all the listed experts, the parties may then instruct ***experts of their own choice****. It would be for the court to decide subsequently, if proceedings are issued, whether either party had acted unreasonably.*

9.8

If the ***second party does not object to an expert nominated****, he shall not be entitled to rely on his own expert evidence within that particular speciality unless:*

1 the first party agrees,
2 the court so directs, or
3 the first party's expert report has been amended and the first party is not prepared to disclose the original report.

9.9

Either party may send to an agreed expert written questions *on the report, relevant to the issues, via the first party's solicitors. The expert should send answers to the questions separately and directly to each party.*

9.10

The cost of a report from an agreed expert will usually be paid by the instructing first party: the costs of the expert replying to questions will usually be borne by the party which asks the questions.

9.11

Where the defendant admits liability in whole or in part, before proceedings are issued, any medical report obtained under this protocol which ***the claimant*** *relies upon, should be disclosed to the other party.*

9.12

Where the defendant obtains a medical report on which he seeks to rely this should be disclosed to the claimant.

9.13

For further guidance see Part 35 of the CPR, Practice Direction 35 and the Protocol for the Instruction of Experts to give Evidence in Civil Claims which is annexed to that Practice Direction.

10 RESOLUTION OF ISSUES

10.1

The Civil Procedure Rules Part 36 enable claimants and defendants to make formal offers to settle before proceedings are started. Parties should consider making such an offer, since to do so often leads to settlement. If such an offer is made, the party making the offer must always supply sufficient evidence and/or information to enable the offer to be properly considered.

10.2

Where a claim is not resolved when the protocol has been followed, the parties might wish to carry out a 'stock take' of the issues in dispute, and the evidence that the court is likely to need to decide those issues, before proceedings are started.

10.3

Prior to proceedings it will be usual for all parties to disclose those expert reports relating to liability and causation upon which they propose to rely.

10.4

The claimant should delay issuing proceedings for 21 days from disclosure of reports to enable the parties to consider whether the claim is capable of settlement.

10.5

Where the defendant is insured and the pre-action steps have been conducted by the insurer, the insurer would normally be expected to nominate solicitors to accept service of proceedings and the claimant's solicitor is recommended to invite the insurer to nominate solicitors to accept service of proceedings and to do so 7-14 days before the intended issue date.

11 LIMITATION

11.1

If by reason of complying with any part of this protocol a claimant's claim may be time-barred under any provision of the Limitation Act 1980, or any other legislation which imposes a time limit for bringing an action, the claimant may commence proceedings without complying with this protocol. In such circumstances, a claimant who commences proceedings without complying with all, or any part, of this protocol may apply to the court on notice for directions as to the timetable and form of procedure to be adopted, at the same time as he requests the court to issue proceedings. The court will consider whether to order a stay of the whole or part of the proceedings pending compliance with this protocol.

Limitation

It is frequently argued by defendants that the claimant had knowledge of his material condition more than three years before bringing the claim and is therefore time barred by virtue of the Limitation Act 1980.

It is certainly true that many claimants do know about their conditions, sometimes up to 10 years or more before bringing the claim. If limitation is pleaded in a Defence it is important to serve a detailed Reply pleading Section 33 of the Limitation Act 1980 including specifying the claimant's date of knowledge on his own case otherwise the claimant will not be able to apply at trial to disapply limitation.

If there is any doubt over the date of knowledge of the claimant proceedings should always be issued earlier rather than later, even if the claimant is within the protocol period. Additionally, it should be remembered that the normal principles of limitation apply to all of these cases including constructive knowledge of the claimant, pursuant to Section 14 of the Limitation Act 1980.

Section 14 and B of the Limitation Act 1980

> ***Special time limit for negligence actions where facts relevant to cause of action are not known at date of accrual.***
>
> *(1) This section applies to any action for damages for negligence, other than one to which section 11 of this Act applies, where the starting date for reckoning the period of limitation under subsection (4)(b) below falls after the date on which the cause of action accrued.*
>
> *(2) Section 2 of this Act shall not apply to an action to which this section applies.*
>
> *(3) An action to which this section applies shall not be brought after the expiration of the period applicable in accordance with subsection (4) below.*
>
> *(4) That period is either—*

(a) six years from the date on which the cause of action accrued; or
(b) three years from the starting date as defined by subsection (5) below, if that period expires later than the period mentioned in paragraph (a) above.

(5) For the purposes of this section, the starting date for reckoning the period of limitation under subsection (4)(b) above is the earliest date on which the plaintiff or any person in whom the cause of action was vested before him first had both the knowledge required for bringing an action for damages in respect of the relevant damage and a right to bring such an action.

(6) In subsection (5) above "the knowledge required for bringing an action for damages in respect of the relevant damage" means knowledge both—
(a) of the material facts about the damage in respect of which damages are claimed; and
(b) of the other facts relevant to the current action mentioned in subsection (8) below.

(7) For the purposes of subsection (6)(a) above, the material facts about the damage are such facts about the damage as would lead a reasonable person who had suffered such damage to consider it sufficiently serious to justify his instituting proceedings for damages against a defendant who did not dispute liability and was able to satisfy a judgment.

(8) The other facts referred to in subsection (6)(b) above are—
(a) that the damage was attributable in whole or in part to the act or omission which is alleged to constitute negligence; and
(b) the identity of the defendant; and
(c) if it is alleged that the act or omission was that of a person other than the defendant, the identity of that person and the additional facts supporting the bringing of an action against the defendant.

(9) Knowledge that any acts or omissions did or did not, as a matter of law, involve negligence is irrelevant for the purposes of subsection (5) above.

(10) For the purposes of this section a person's knowledge includes knowledge which he might reasonably have been expected to acquire —

(a) from facts observable or ascertainable by him; or
(b) from facts ascertainable by him with the help of appropriate expert advice which it is reasonable for him to seek;
but a person shall not be taken by virtue of this subsection to have knowledge of a fact ascertainable only with the help of expert advice so long as he has taken all reasonable steps to obtain (and, where appropriate, to act on) that advice.

Section 33 of the Limitation Act 1980

Discretionary exclusion of time limit for actions in respect of personal injuries or death

(1) If it appears to the court that it would be equitable to allow an action to proceed having regard to the degree to which—
(a) the provisions of section 11 [F48or 11A] or 12 of this Act prejudice the plaintiff or any person whom he represents; and
(b) any decision of the court under this subsection would prejudice the defendant or any person whom he represents; the court may direct that those provisions shall not apply to the action, or shall not apply to any specified cause of action to which the action relates.

[F49(1A)The court shall not under this section disapply—
(a) subsection (3) of section 11A; or
(b) where the damages claimed by the plaintiff are confined to damages for loss of or damage to any property, any other provision in its application to an action by virtue of Part I of the M11 Consumer Protection Act 1987.]

(2) The court shall not under this section disapply section 12(1) except where the reason why the person injured could no longer maintain an action was because of the time limit in section 11 [F50or subsection (4) of section 11A].If, for example, the person injured could at his death no longer maintain an action under the M12Fatal Accidents Act 1976 because of the time limit in Article 29

in Schedule 1 to the M13Carriage by Air Act 1961, the court has no power to direct that section 12(1) shall not apply.

(3) In acting under this section the court shall have regard to all the circumstances of the case and in particular to—
(a) the length of, and the reasons for, the delay on the part of the plaintiff;
(b) the extent to which, having regard to the delay, the evidence adduced or likely to be adduced by the plaintiff or the defendant is or is likely to be less cogent than if the action had been brought within the time allowed by section 11 [F51, by section 11A] or (as the case may be) by section 12;
(c) the conduct of the defendant after the cause of action arose, including the extent (if any) to which he responded to requests reasonably made by the plaintiff for information or inspection for the purpose of ascertaining facts which were or might be relevant to the plaintiff's cause of action against the defendant;
(d) the duration of any disability of the plaintiff arising after the date of the accrual of the cause of action;
(e) the extent to which the plaintiff acted promptly and reasonably once he knew whether or not the act or omission of the defendant, to which the injury was attributable, might be capable at that time of giving rise to an action for damages;
(f) the steps, if any, taken by the plaintiff to obtain medical, legal or other expert advice and the nature of any such advice he may have received.

(4) In a case where the person injured died when, because of section 11 [F50or subsection (4) of section 11A], he could no longer maintain an action and recover damages in respect of the injury, the court shall have regard in particular to the length of, and the reasons for, the delay on the part of the deceased.

(5) In a case under subsection (4) above, or any other case where the time limit, or one of the time limits, depends on the date of knowledge of a person other than the plaintiff, subsection (3) above shall have effect with appropriate modifications, and shall have effect in particular as if references to the plaintiff included references to any

person whose date of knowledge is or was relevant in determining a time limit.

(6) A direction by the court disapplying the provisions of section 12(1) shall operate to disapply the provisions to the same effect in section 1(1) of the M14Fatal Accidents Act 1976.

(7) In this section "the court" means the court in which the action has been brought.

(8) References in this section to section 11 [F52or 11A] include references to that section as extended by any of the [F53provisions of this Part of this Act other than this section] or by any provision of Part III of this Act.

The authors between them have extensive experience of limitation trials and that experience indicates that defendants often focus on constructive knowledge and, consequently, claimant's witness statement should set out very clearly why the claimant did not link his disease to his workplace when he is now making positive allegations of breach of duty regarding that workplace. In a noise claim, for example, the claimant will be cross-examined for a prolonged period - often for up to 2 hours or more.

CHAPTER TWO
THE PORTALS AND FIXED COSTS

The Low Value Portal in Employers' Liability Claims Came into effect for any claim where the accident date is on or after 31 July 2013. The purpose of this Chapter is to examine the most important aspects of those Portals in the context of Low Value Personal Injury claims and claims that start off with the Low Value Portal but then exit the Portal.

The Portals can be found at:- http://www.justice.gov.uk/courts/procedure-rules/civil/protocol/pre-action-protocol-for-low-value-personal-injury-employers-liability-and-public-liability-claims#2.1

Which types of claims does the Portal apply to?

Paragraph 4.1 of the Portal helpfully sets out which claims they apply to:-

> *4.1 This Protocol applies where—*
>
> *(1) Either—*
>
> *(a) the claim arises from an accident occurring on or after 31 July 2013; or*
> ***(b) in a disease claim, no letter of claim has been sent to the defendant before 31 July 2013;***
>
> *(2) the claim includes damages in respect of personal injury;*
>
> *(3) the claimant values the claim at not more than £25,000 on a full liability basis including pecuniary losses but excluding interest ('the upper limit'); and*
>
> *(4) if proceedings were started the small claims track would not be the normal track for that claim.*

It is important to note that if the claim is valued at more than £25,000 on a full liability basis, the claim will not commence in the Low Value Portal. It is also helpful that the Protocol ceases to apply to a claim where, at any stage, the claimant notifies the defendant that the claim has now been revalued at more than the upper limit. Some Solicitors make the mistake of thinking that the Low Value Portal applies to accidents before 31 July 2013, and it is important to note it does not, and any accidents before this date, will still attract costs on the standard basis.

Claims to which the Low Value Portal does not apply

There are a large number of scenarios where the Low Value Portal will not apply, and these are set out as follows:-

> *4.3 This Protocol does not apply to a claim—*
>
> *(1) where the claimant or defendant acts as personal representative of a deceased person;*
>
> *(2) where the claimant or defendant is a protected party as defined in rule 21.1(2);*
>
> *(3) in the case of a public liability claim, where the defendant is an individual ('individual' does not include a defendant who is sued in their business capacity or in their capacity as an office holder);*
>
> *(4) where the claimant is bankrupt;*
>
> ***(5) where the defendant is insolvent and there is no identifiable insurer;***
>
> ***(6) in the case of a disease claim, where there is more than one employer defendant;***
>
> *(7) for personal injury arising from an accident or alleged breach of duty occurring outside England and Wales;*

(8) for damages in relation to harm, abuse or neglect of or by children or vulnerable adults;

(9) which includes a claim for clinical negligence;

(10) for mesothelioma;

(11) for damages arising out of a road traffic accident (as defined in paragraph 1.1(16) of the Pre-Action Protocol for Low Value Personal Injury Claims in Road Traffic Accidents).

Mesothelioma cases do not start inside the Low Value Portal, arguably due to their complexity. Similarly, where there is a disease case with more than one Defendant, this will also not start inside the Low Value Portal. Further it may be important to note that the Protocol does not apply where the Defendant is an individual in the case of a public liability claim, or the defendant is insolvent and there is no identifiable insurer.

The Claim Notification Form ('CNF')

The Protocol sets out the following stages for completion of the CNF:-

Stage 1: Completion of the Claim Notification Form

6.1

(1) The claimant must complete and send—
(a) the CNF to the defendant's insurer, if known; and
(b) the Defendant Only Claim Notification Form ("Defendant Only CNF") to the defendant,
but the requirement to send the form to the defendant may be ignored in a disease claim where the CNF has been sent to the insurer and the defendant has been dissolved, is insolvent or has ceased to trade.

(2) If—

(a) the insurer's identity is not known; or
(b) the defendant is known not to hold insurance cover,
the CNF must be sent to the defendant's registered office or principal place of business and no Defendant Only CNF is required.

(3) Where the insurer's identity is not known, the claimant must make a reasonable attempt to identify the insurer and, in an employers' liability claim, the claimant must have carried out a database search through the Employers' Liability Tracing Office.

(4) In a disease claim, the CNF should be sent to the insurer identified as the insurer last on risk for the employer for the material period of employment.

6.2

If the CNF or Defendant Only CNF cannot be sent to the defendant via the prescribed Portal address, it must be sent via first class post; and this must be done, in a case where the CNF is sent to the insurer, at the same time or as soon as practicable after the CNF is sent.

6.3

All boxes in the CNF that are marked as mandatory must be completed before it is sent. The claimant must make a reasonable attempt to complete those boxes that are not marked as mandatory.

6.4

Where the claimant is a child, this must be noted in the relevant section of the CNF.

6.5

The statement of truth in the CNF must be signed either by the claimant or by the claimant's legal representative where the claimant has authorised the legal representative to do so and the

legal representative can produce written evidence of that authorisation. Where the claimant is a child the statement of truth may be signed by the parent or guardian. On the electronically completed CNF the person may enter their name in the signature box to satisfy this requirement.

There are a number of significant points that arise from this. Firstly the claimant Solicitor must ensure that the before the CNF is signed, it is sent to the Claimant to check and the Claimant's Solicitor must have written confirmation from the Claimant that the CNF has been agreed. This can be requested by the Defendant's insurer later on in the proceedings. An important part of this process, is that all too often at Trial, the information on the CNF is incorrect, which can affect the credibility of the claim at Trial, especially as regards to the mechanism of the accident, and that is why it is essential that the Claimant gets an opportunity to check the CNF before it is submitted to the Defendant's insurer, and make any corrections that are required.

Secondly, sometimes a situation arises where there is no identifiable insurer. The Portal rules require that a search is made of the *Employers' Liability Tracing Office*. The website to undertake the search can be found at:- https://eld.elto.org.uk/TCUsage/TANDC

Thirdly, as with other types of claims, all the mandatory information on the CNF must be completed. There is a warning in the Protocol which sets out:-

6.7 - Failure to complete the Claim Notification Form

Where the defendant considers that inadequate mandatory information has been provided in the CNF that shall be a valid reason for the defendant to decide that the claim should no longer continue under this Protocol.

6.8

Rule 45.24(2) sets out the sanctions available to the court where it considers that the claimant provided inadequate information in the CNF.

Exit Points from the Portal

6.13 - Contributory Negligence, liability not admitted or failure to respond

The claim will no longer continue under this Protocol where the defendant, within the relevant period in paragraph 6.11 —

(1) makes an admission of liability but alleges contributory negligence;

(2) does not complete and send the CNF response;

(3) does not admit liability; or

(4) notifies the claimant that the defendant considers that—
(a) there is inadequate mandatory information in the CNF; or
(b) if proceedings were issued, the small claims track would be the normal track for that claim.

6.14

Where the defendant does not admit liability, the defendant must give brief reasons in the CNF response.

6.15

Where paragraph 6.13 applies the claim will proceed under the relevant Pre-Action Protocol and the CNF will serve as the letter of claim (except where the claim no longer continues under this Protocol because the CNF contained inadequate information). Time will be treated as running under the relevant Pre-Action Protocol from the date the form of acknowledgment is served under paragraph 6.9 or 6.10.

There are therefore a number of ways in which the claim can exit the Portal. It is important for Claimant Solicitors to note the exit points from the Portal and provide appropriate notification to the insurer where an exit point is reached. It is helpful if the Claimant Lawyer has a suitable claims management system that will provide a notification of, for example, the expiration of the time-limit for investigations, whether an admission has been made and/or other potential points of exit from the Portal.

Time Limits

6.11

The defendant must complete the 'Response' section of the CNF ("the CNF response") and send it to the claimant—

(a) in the case of an employers' liability claim, within 30 days of the step taken pursuant to paragraph 6.1;

Notwithstanding the above, one may often find in practice, that given the complexity of these types of cases, the employer and/or their insurer will not be able to realistically investigate the cases within 30 days, and this can be one of the reasons for the high drop-out rates from the Low Value Portal.

Admissions in the Portal

1.1 In this Protocol—

(1) 'admission of liability' means the defendant admits that—

(a) the breach of duty occurred;

(b) the defendant thereby caused some loss to the claimant, the nature and extent of which is not admitted; and

(c) the defendant has no accrued defence to the claim under the Limitation Act 1980;

It should be noted that if an admission is made, and the Defendant then later exits the Portal, the admission will still be binding, unless the Courts permission is sought to withdraw the admission post proceedings or consent is provided. CPR 14.1B says:-

14.1B - Admissions made under the RTA Protocol or the EL/PL Protocol

(1) This rule applies to a pre-action admission made in a case to which the Pre-Action Protocol for Low Value Personal Injury Claims in Road Traffic Accidents ('the RTA Protocol') or the Pre-action Protocol for Low Value Personal Injury (Employers' Liability and Public Liability) Claims ('the EL/PL Protocol') applies.

(2) The defendant may, by giving notice in writing withdraw an admission of causation –
(a) before commencement of proceedings –
(i) during the initial consideration period (or any extension to that period) as defined in the relevant Protocol; or
(ii) at any time if the person to whom the admission was made agrees; or
(b) after commencement of proceedings –
(i) if all the parties to the proceedings consent; or
(ii) with the permission of the court.

(3) The defendant may, by giving notice in writing withdraw any other pre-action admission after commencement of proceedings –
(a) if all the parties to the proceedings consent; or
(b) with the permission of the court.

(4) An application under rule 14.1B(2)(b)(ii) or (3)(b) to withdraw a pre-action admission must be made in accordance with Part 23.

Portal Costs and Disbursements – claims which remain in Portal

Fixed costs in relation to the EL/PL Protocol			
Where the value of the claim for damages is not more than £10,000		Where the value of the claim for damages is more than £10,000, but not more than £25,000	
Stage 1 fixed costs	£300	Stage 1 fixed costs	£300
Stage 2 fixed costs	£600	Stage 2 fixed costs	£1300
Stage 3 - Type A fixed costs	£250	Stage 3 - Type A fixed costs	£250
Stage 3 - Type B fixed costs	£250	Stage 3 - Type B fixed costs	£250
Stage 3 - Type C fixed costs	£150	Stage 3 - Type C fixed costs	£150

The Fixed costs raises real questions of access to Justice and how Low Value Claims can be run in a fixed costs environment. Some points to consider are:-

a) To ensure that the correct level of fee earner is undertaking the work. There is now little point in Grade A fee earners undertaking Low Value cases. The majority of Portal cases now calls for Paralegals to undertake the work to make it efficient.

b) To ensure that more experienced fee earners are undertaking the higher value and more complex portal cases. In this respect, one has to be cautious to ensure that the fee earner undertaking the work has appropriate supervision. It is a common misconception that dealing with portal work is straightforward and it must be borne in mind that £25,000 personal injury claims, if litigated, could be in the multi-track.

c) To ensure that you have a case management system for Portal Cases. This is particularly useful for keeping matters running efficiently and exiting claims from the Portal. Proclaim's A2A software is very efficient for Low Value Portal routine cases, and the package of letters includes all the relevant correspondence, which is required when working to very tight fees.

Disbursements in the Portal

45.19

(1) Subject to paragraphs (2A) to (2E), the court –
(a) may allow a claim for a disbursement of a type mentioned in paragraphs (2) or (3); but
(b) will not allow a claim for any other type of disbursement.

(2) In a claim to which either the RTA Protocol or EL/PL Protocol applies, the disbursements referred to in paragraph (1) are –
(a) the cost of obtaining –
(i) medical records;
(ii) a medical report or reports or non-medical expert reports as provided for in the relevant Protocol;
(aa) Driver Vehicle Licensing Authority;
(bb) Motor Insurance Database;
(b) court fees as a result of Part 21 being applicable;
(c) court fees payable where proceedings are started as a result of a limitation period that is about to expire;
(d) court fees in respect of the Stage 3 Procedure; and
(e) any other disbursement that has arisen due to a particular feature of the dispute.

(2A) In a soft tissue injury claim to which the RTA Protocol applies, the only sums (exclusive of VAT) that are recoverable in respect of the

cost of obtaining a fixed cost medical report or medical records are as follows—
(a) obtaining the first report from an accredited medical expert selected via the MedCo Portal: £180;
(b) obtaining a further report where justified from an expert from one of the following disciplines—
(i) Consultant Orthopaedic Surgeon (inclusive of a review of medical records where applicable): £420;
(ii) Consultant in Accident and Emergency Medicine: £360;
(iii) General Practitioner registered with the General Medical Council: £180; or
(iv) Physiotherapist registered with the Health and Care Professions Council: £180;
(c) obtaining medical records: no more than £30 plus the direct cost from the holder of the records, and limited to £80 in total for each set of records required. Where relevant records are required from more than one holder of records, the fixed fee applies to each set of records required;
(d) addendum report on medical records (except by Consultant Orthopaedic Surgeon): £50; and
(e) answer to questions under Part 35: £80.

Interim Payments in the Portal

It may be argued that where one has a seriously injured client, for example a longstanding condition where the claim remains in the Portal, the Claimant should always be advised to wait until the end of the prognosis period before settling the claim, to see if he or she recovers in accordance with the prognosis period in the medical report. However, many Claimants, against advice, will often seek to take the money, as they need it because the accident has caused financial hardship. An interim payment can become incredibly useful in such circumstances, whilst the Claimant waits to see how the injuries settle down and to ensure the Claimant is recovered before a claim is settled.

The rules set out as follows:-

Request for an interim payment

7.12

Where the claimant requests an interim payment of £1,000, the defendant should make an interim payment to the claimant in accordance with paragraph 7.17.

7.13

The claimant must send to the defendant the Interim Settlement Pack and initial medical reports (including any recommendation that a subsequent medical report is justified) in order to request the interim payment.

7.14

The claimant must also send evidence of pecuniary losses and disbursements. This will assist the defendant in considering whether to make an offer to settle the claim.

7.15

Where an interim payment of more than £1,000 is requested the claimant must specify in the Interim Settlement Pack the amount requested, the heads of damage which are the subject of the request and the reasons for the request.

7.16

Unless the parties agree otherwise—

(a) the interim payment of £1,000 is only in relation to general damages; and
(b) where more than £1,000 is requested by the claimant, the amount in excess of £1,000 is only in relation to pecuniary losses.

7.17

(1) Where paragraph 7.12 applies the defendant must pay £1,000 within 10 days of receiving the Interim Settlement Pack.

(2) Sub-paragraph (1) does not apply in a claim in respect of a disease to which the Pneumoconiosis etc. (Workers' Compensation) Act 1979 applies unless there is a valid CRU certificate showing no deduction for recoverable lump sum payments.

Interim payment of more than £1,000

7.18

Subject to paragraphs 7.19 and 7.21, where the claimant has requested an interim payment of more than £1,000 the defendant must pay—

(1) the full amount requested less any deductible amount which is payable to the CRU;

(2) the amount of £1,000; or

(3) some other amount of more than £1,000 but less than the amount requested by the claimant,
within 15 days of receiving the Interim Settlement Pack.

7.19

Where a payment is made under paragraphs 7.18(2) or (3) the defendant must briefly explain in the Interim Settlement Pack why the full amount requested by the claimant is not agreed.

7.20

Where the claim is valued at more than £10,000, the claimant may use the procedure at paragraphs 7.12 to 7.19 to request more than one interim payment.

7.21

Nothing in this Protocol is intended to affect the provisions contained in the Rehabilitation Code.

It should be borne in mind that this process may only be utilised where there is a need for a further report. If the Defendant fails to make the interim payment, the Claimant may exit the claim from the process, subject to the following provisions:-

7.26

Where the defendant does not comply with paragraphs 7.17 or 7.18 the claimant may start proceedings under Part 7 of the CPR and apply to the court for an interim payment in those proceedings.

7.27

Where the defendant does comply with paragraph 7.18(2) or (3) but the claimant is not content with the amount paid, the claimant may still start proceedings. However, the court will order the defendant to pay no more than the Stage 2 fixed costs where the court awards an interim payment of no more than the amount offered by the defendant or the court makes no award.

7.28

Where paragraph 7.26 or 7.27 applies the claimant must give notice to the defendant that the claim will no longer continue under this Protocol. Unless the claimant's notice is sent to the defendant within 10 days after the expiry of the period in paragraphs 7.17, 7.18 or 7.23 as appropriate, the claim will continue under this Protocol.

Fixed Costs and Disbursements – Claims which Exit the Portal

Fixed costs where a claim no longer continues under the EL/PL Protocol – employers' liability claims			
A. If Parties reach a settlement prior to the claimant issuing proceedings under Part 7			
Agreed damages	At least £1,000, but not more than £5,000	More than £5,000, but not more than £10,000	More than £10,000, but not more than £25,000
Fixed costs	The total of— (a) £950; and (b) 17.5% of the damages	The total of— (a) £1,855; and (b) 12.5% of damages over £5,000	The total of — (a) £2,500; and (b) 10% of damages over £10,000
B. If proceedings are issued under Part 7, but the case settles before trial			
Stage at which case is settled	On or after the date of issue, but prior to the date of allocation under Part 26	On or after the date of allocation under Part 26, but prior to the date of listing	On or after the date of listing but prior the date of trial

<table>
<tr><td>Fixed costs</td><td>The total of—
(a) £2,630; and
(b) 20% of the damages</td><td>The total of—
(a) £3,350; and
(b) 25% of the damages</td><td colspan="2">The total of —
(a) £4,280; and
(b) 30% of the damages</td></tr>
<tr><td colspan="5">C. If the claim is disposed of at trial</td></tr>
<tr><td>Fixed costs</td><td colspan="4">The total of—
(a) £4,280;
(b) 30% of the damages agreed or awarded; and
(c) the relevant trial advocacy fee</td></tr>
<tr><td colspan="5">D. Trial advocacy fees</td></tr>
<tr><td>Damages agreed or awarded</td><td>Not more than £3,000</td><td>More than £3,000, but not more than £10,000</td><td>More than £10,000, but not more than £15,000</td><td>More than £15,000</td></tr>
<tr><td>Trial advocacy fee</td><td>£500</td><td>£710</td><td>£1,070</td><td>£1,705</td></tr>
<tr><td colspan="5"></td></tr>
</table>

Disbursements for Claims within Fixed Recoverable Costs

45.29I

(1) Subject to paragraphs (2A) to (2E), the court—
(a) may allow a claim for a disbursement of a type mentioned in paragraphs (2) or (3); but
(b) will not allow a claim for any other type of disbursement.

(2) In a claim started under either the RTA Protocol or the EL/PL Protocol, the disbursements referred to in paragraph (1) are—
(a) the cost of obtaining medical records and expert medical reports as provided for in the relevant Protocol;
(b) the cost of any non-medical expert reports as provided for in the relevant Protocol;
(c) the cost of any advice from a specialist solicitor or counsel as provided for in the relevant Protocol;
(d) court fees;
(e) any expert's fee for attending the trial where the court has given permission for the expert to attend;
(f) expenses which a party or witness has reasonably incurred in travelling to and from a hearing or in staying away from home for the purposes of attending a hearing;
(g) a sum not exceeding the amount specified in Practice Direction 45 for any loss of earnings or loss of leave by a party or witness due to attending a hearing or to staying away from home for the purpose of attending a hearing; and
(h) any other disbursement reasonably incurred due to a particular feature of the dispute.

(2A) In a soft tissue injury claim started under the RTA Protocol, the only sums (exclusive of VAT) that are recoverable in respect of the cost of obtaining a fixed cost medical report or medical records are as follows—
(a) obtaining the first report from an accredited medical expert selected via the MedCo Portal: £180;
(b) obtaining a further report where justified from an expert from one of the following disciplines—

(i) Consultant Orthopaedic Surgeon (inclusive of a review of medical records where applicable): £420;
(ii) Consultant in Accident and Emergency Medicine: £360;
(iii) General Practitioner registered with the General Medical Council: £180; or
(iv) Physiotherapist registered with the Health and Care Professions Council: £180;
(c) obtaining medical records: no more than £30 plus the direct cost from the holder of the records, and limited to £80 in total for each set of records required. Where relevant records are required from more than one holder of records, the fixed fee applies to each set of records required;
(d) addendum report on medical records (except by Consultant Orthopaedic Surgeon): £50; and
(e) answer to questions under Part 35: £80.

(2B) Save in exceptional circumstances, no fee may be allowed for the cost of obtaining a report to which paragraph (2A) applies where the medical expert—
(a) has provided treatment to the claimant;
(b) is associated with any person who has provided treatment; or
(c) proposes or recommends treatment that they or an associate then provide.

(2C) The cost of obtaining a further report from an expert not listed in paragraph (2A)(b) is not fixed, but the use of that expert and the cost must be justified.

What about interlocutory applications?

The costs recovery of interlocutory applications has now become very limited and is set out in CPR 45 as follows:-

45.29H - Interim applications

(1) Where the court makes an order for costs of an interim application to be paid by one party in a case to which this Section applies,

> ***the order shall be for a sum equivalent to one half of the applicable Type A and Type B costs in Table 6 or 6A.***
>
> *(2) Where the party in whose favour the order for costs is made—*
> *(a) lives, works or carries on business in an area set out in Practice Direction 45; and*
> *(b) instructs a legal representative who practises in that area,*
> *the costs will include, in addition to the costs allowable under paragraph (1), an amount equal to 12.5% of those costs.*
>
> *(3) If an order for costs is made pursuant to this rule, the party in whose favour the order is made is entitled to disbursements in accordance with rule 45.29I.*
>
> *(4) Where appropriate, VAT may be recovered in addition to the amount of any costs allowable under this rule.*

Complex Cases – Amount of Costs Exceeding Fixed Recoverable Costs

There is scope within the rules for a claim for an amount exceeding fixed recoverable costs or predictive costs, where there are 'exceptional circumstances', and it is set out as follows:-

> *45.13 - Claims for an amount of costs exceeding fixed recoverable costs*
>
> *(1) The court will entertain a claim for an amount of costs (excluding any success fee or disbursements) greater than the fixed recoverable costs but only if it considers that there are* ***exceptional circumstances*** *making it appropriate to do so.*
>
> *(2) If the court considers such a claim appropriate, it may –*
> *(a) summarily assess the costs; or*
> *(b) make an order for the costs to be subject to detailed assessment.*

(3) If the court does not consider the claim appropriate, it will make an order for fixed recoverable costs (and any permitted disbursements) only.

There is no current definition in the White Book, as to what this is likely to mean in practice, However, from experience this is likely to potentially apply in the following examples:-

a) a multi party claim

b) a serious injury claim, which for whatever reason is not allocated to the multi-track.

c) Allegations of fraud, with volumes of disclosure.

However, if the application is made and fails, the following consequences will apply:-

45.14

(1) This rule applies where –
(a) costs are assessed in accordance with rule 45.13(2); and
(b) the court assesses the costs (excluding any VAT) as being an amount which is less than 20% greater than the amount of the fixed recoverable costs.

(2) The court must order the defendant to pay to the claimant the lesser of –
(a) the fixed recoverable costs; and
(b) the assessed costs.

<u>Solicitor CFAs Post-April 2013</u>

As part of this Chapter it is helpful to note the provisions for Conditional Fee Agreements, post April 2013 and success fees, from the Claimant, post-April 2013. They are set out as follows in LASPO 2012:-

44 - Conditional fee agreements: success fees

(4B) The additional conditions are that—
(a) the agreement must provide that the success fee is subject to a maximum limit,
(b) the maximum limit must be expressed as a percentage of the descriptions of damages awarded in the proceedings that are specified in the agreement,
(c) that percentage must not exceed the percentage specified by order made by the Lord Chancellor in relation to the proceedings or calculated in a manner so specified, and
(d) those descriptions of damages may only include descriptions of damages specified by order made by the Lord Chancellor in relation to the proceedings."

This should be read in conjunction with the Conditional Fee Agreements Order 2013, which sets out:-

Specified proceedings

4. A claim for personal injuries shall be proceedings specified for the purpose of section 58(4A)(b) of the Act.

Amount of success fee in specified proceedings

5. (1) In relation to the proceedings specified in article 4, the percentage prescribed for the purposes of section 58(4B)(c) of the Act is—
(a) in proceedings at first instance, 25%; and
(b) in all other proceedings, 100%.

(2) The descriptions of damages specified for the purposes of section 58(4B)(d) of the Act are—
(a) general damages for pain, suffering, and loss of amenity; and
(b) damages for pecuniary loss, other than future pecuniary loss,
net of any sums recoverable by the Compensation Recovery Unit of the Department for Work and Pensions.

Thus, in post-April 2013 proceedings, the rules suggest that the Solicitor can charge the Claimant 25% of past pecuniary losses and general damages recovered, **but not** future losses and thus the explanatory note sets out in the order:-

> *Notwithstanding the effect of article 3, section 58(4B) of the 1990 Act, enables the Lord Chancellor, in respect of proceedings specified by order under section 58(4A), to effectively cap the lawyer's success fee at a percentage of specified damages awarded to the client.* ***Article 5 provides that, in a claim for personal injuries, the success fee shall be limited to a maximum of 25% of the damages awarded for pain, suffering and loss of amenity and pecuniary loss, other than future pecuniary loss and net of any sums recoverable by the Compensation Recovery Unit, inclusive of VAT.***

Qualified One Way Costs Shifting (QOCS)

Pre-action disclosure applications are not protected by QOCS, nor are proceedings where a claimant has entered into a pre-commencement funding arrangement, which is defined in:-

> *48.2(1)*
>
> *A pre-commencement funding arrangement is-*
>
> *(i) a funding arrangement as defined by rule 43.2(1)(k)(i) where……"*
>
> *CPR 43.2(1)(k)(i) defines a funding arrangement as "an arrangement where a person has –*
>
> *(i) entered into a conditional fee agreement or a collective conditional fee agreement which provides for a success fee….."*

The QOCS rules set out under 44.14:-

Effect of qualified one-way costs shifting

44.14

(1) Subject to rules 44.15 and 44.16, ***orders for costs made against a claimant may be enforced without the permission of the court but only to the extent that the aggregate amount in money terms of such orders does not exceed the aggregate amount in money terms of any orders for damages and interest made in favour of the claimant.***

(2) ***Orders for costs made against a claimant may only be enforced after the proceedings have been concluded and the costs have been assessed or agreed.***

(3) ***An order for costs which is enforced only to the extent permitted by paragraph (1) shall not be treated as an unsatisfied or outstanding judgment for the purposes of any court record.***

Exceptions to qualified one-way costs shifting where permission not required

44.15 Orders for costs made against the claimant may be enforced to the full extent of such orders without the permission of the court where the proceedings have been struck out on the grounds that –
(a) the claimant has disclosed no reasonable grounds for bringing the proceedings;
(b) the proceedings are an abuse of the court's process; or
(c) the conduct of –
(i) the claimant; or
(ii) a person acting on the claimant's behalf and with the claimant's knowledge of such conduct,
is likely to obstruct the just disposal of the proceedings.

Exceptions to qualified one-way costs shifting where permission required

> *44.16*
>
> ***(1) Orders for costs made against the claimant may be enforced to the full extent of such orders with the permission of the court where the claim is found on the balance of probabilities to be fundamentally dishonest.***

In order words, if the Claimant proceeds to Trial, and recovers zero, provided that the claim is not found to be fundamentally dishonest, or one of the other exemptions above applies, the Court can still make a costs order, but the Defendant will not be able to enforce it. A County Court Judgment would not be recorded against the Claimant in such circumstances.

The Defendant will only, in summary, be able to enforce any order up to the amount of damages recovered by the Claimant.

QOCS protection may however be lost if the claimant fails to beat a defendant's Part 36 offer, but the defendant will only be able to recover costs up to the level of the claimant's damages. QOCS, of course, took away much of the need for After the Event insurance cover in relation to low value personal injury cases in some circumstances, as in effect the Claimant's risk of paying the Defendant's costs has now been taken away except in very limited circumstances.

Claimant Lawyers have to be wary of the rules surrounding fundamental dishonesty. In the case of *Gosling v Screwfix and Anr* (unreported, 29 March 2014) at Cambridge County Court, HHJ Moloney QC ordered the claimant to pay the defendant's costs of the action on an indemnity basis. The Judge ruled that a personal injury claimant who exaggerated the extent of his ongoing symptoms should be denied the protection of qualified one-way costs shifting on the grounds that the claim was "fundamentally dishonest."

Caution should be expressed in multiple defendant cases, where it is arguable that QOCS protection may not apply against a Defendant who is sued in a multiple defendant case, and the case fails against that Defendant. QOCS arguably allows recovery of costs by the Defendant against whom the Claimant has failed up to the aggregate amount of damages awarded to the Claimant. In such circumstances, a *Sanderson* or *Bullock* order should be sought that the compensating Defendant pay the costs Order, and the Claimant should take ATE to cover such a risk.

Defendant's Costs and Part 36 Offers – Post-July 2013 Cases

Defendant's Costs can recovered in certain circumstances within FRC and CPR 45 sets out as follows:-

45.29F

(1) In this rule—
(c) paragraphs (2) to (7) apply to all other cases under this Section in which a defendant's costs are assessed.

(2) If, in any case to which this Section applies, the court makes an order for costs in favour of the defendant—
(a) the court will have regard to; and
(b) the amount of costs order to be paid shall not exceed,
the amount which would have been payable by the defendant if an order for costs had been made in favour of the claimant at the same stage of the proceedings.

(3) For the purpose of assessing the costs payable to the defendant by reference to the fixed costs in Table 6, Table 6A, Table 6B, Table 6C and Table 6D, "value of the claim for damages" and "damages" shall be treated as references to the value of the claim.

(4) For the purposes of paragraph (3), "the value of the claim" is —

(a) the amount specified in the claim form, excluding—
(i) any amount not in dispute;
(ii) in a claim started under the RTA Protocol, any claim for vehicle related damages;
(iii) interest;

(iv) costs; and
(v) any contributory negligence;
(b) if no amount is specified in the claim form, the maximum amount which the claimant reasonably expected to recover according to the statement of value included in the claim form under rule 16.3; or
(c) £25,000, if the claim form states that the claimant cannot reasonably say how much is likely to be recovered.

(6) Where an order for costs is made pursuant to this rule, the defendant is entitled to disbursements in accordance with rule 45.29I

(7) Where appropriate, VAT may be recovered in addition to the amount of any costs allowable under this rule.

Thus for the purpose of the assessment exercise, the Defendant can only recover its fixed costs that would have been payable by the Defendant, to the Claimant, if an order for costs had been made in favour of the Claimant at the same stage in the proceedings.

The Defendant can still of course make a Part 36 offers within proceedings to protect its costs position, and the following provisions will apply:-

Where the claimant accepts an offer after the relevant period has elapsed, or the defendant achieves judgment more favorable than its offer:

- the claimant will recover costs calculated based on the stage when the relevant period elapsed and the value of damages recovered
- the claimant will be liable for the defendant's costs for the period from the date of expiry of the relevant period to the date of acceptance
- if the parties do not agree the liability for costs then the court will make the determination
- in relation to the defendant's costs the sum awarded by the court "***shall not exceed the fixed costs….applicable at the date of acceptance, less the fixed costs to which the claimant is entitled***".

The Claimant can make early Part 36 offers in FRC cases and the consequences for the Defendant in the Claimant obtaining a more advantageous Judgment at Trial, are it can be argued, quite severe for the Defendant:-

36.14

(1) Subject to rule 36.14A, this rule applies where upon judgment being entered –
(a) a claimant fails to obtain a judgment more advantageous than a defendant's Part 36 offer; or
(b) judgment against the defendant is at least as advantageous to the claimant as the proposals contained in a claimant's Part 36 offer.

(1A) For the purposes of paragraph (1), in relation to any money claim or money element of a claim, 'more advantageous' means better in money terms by any amount, however small, and 'at least as advantageous' shall be construed accordingly.

(2) Subject to paragraphs (6) and (7), where rule 36.14(1)(a) applies, the court will, unless it considers it unjust to do so, order that the defendant is entitled to:
(a) costs from the date on which the relevant period expired; and
(b) interest on those costs.

(3) Subject to paragraph (6), where rule 36.14(1)(b) applies, the court will, unless it considers it unjust to do so, order that the claimant is entitled to –
(a) interest on the whole or part of any sum of money (excluding interest) awarded at a rate not exceeding 10% above base rate[(GL)] for some or all of the period starting with the date on which the relevant period expired;
(b) his costs on the indemnity basis from the date on which the relevant period expired; and
(c) interest on those costs at a rate not exceeding 10% above base rate[(GL)]; and

(d) an additional amount, which shall not exceed £75,000, calculated by applying the prescribed percentage set out below to an amount which is
(i) where the claim is or includes a money claim, the sum awarded to the claimant by the court; or
(ii) where the claim is only a non-monetary claim, the sum awarded to the claimant by the court in respect of costs –

Amount awarded by the court	*Prescribed percentage*
up to £500,000	*10% of the amount awarded;*
above £500,000 up to £1,000,000	*10% of the first £500,000 and 5% of any amount above that figure*

It is argued that it is therefore prudent for Claimant lawyers to make early Part 36 offers to encourage Defendants to settle early. This will likely be the only way, it can be argued that Defendants will be encouraged to settle cases within fixed recoverable costs. Early and realistic Part 36 offers will hold a tactical advantage for the Claimant.

A Warning for Disease Cases and Multiple Defendants

In *Cartwright v Venduct Engineering Ltd* [2018] EWCA Civ 1654, the claimant issued proceedings against six named defendants for noise induced hearing loss (NIHL). The third defendant, Venduct, accepted that it was responsible for any liability that was established on the part of the first and second defendants.

The claimant then settled with the fourth, fifth and sixth defendants, who agreed to pay him £20,000. This was recorded in a Tomlin order. The claimant then served a notice of discontinuance in respect of the claim against Venduct. Venduct then sought its costs of £8,000 from the claimant; under the QOCS rule 44.14(1), a successful defendant can enforce a costs order up to the damages recovered by the claimant.

At first instance, Regional Costs Judge Hale in Nottingham held that the Tomlin order did not meet the requirement of the rule that such costs could only be paid from an "*order for damages and interest. The schedule to a Tomlin order was not an order of the court*", he said. However, he also ruled that Venduct would have been entitled under rule 44.14, in principle, to enforce its costs order against the claimant, even though the source of the claimant's funds was another defendant. The Court said:-

> 22.*For the reasons explained below, I consider that each of these ways of testing the underlying dispute between the parties about multi-defendant cases leads to the conclusion that the Costs Judge was correct when he concluded that Venduct were, in principle, entitled to enforce its costs order against the claimant, even though the source of the claimant's funds was another defendant.*
>
> 23.*Let us assume that the claimant issued proceedings against two defendants, A and B, which went all the way to trial. The claimant recovered £100,000 against defendant A, but the claim against defendant B failed, leading B to incur £40,000 by way of costs. In circumstances where the claimant had freely sued B (so that a Bullock or Sanderson order was inappropriate), I can see no reason in principle why B should not recover the £40,000 from the £100,000 payable by A to the claimant.*
>
> 24.***The QOWCS regime is designed to ensure that a claimant does not incur a net liability as a result of his or her personal injury claim: that, at worst, he or she has broken even at the end of the action. In the example I have given, the QOWCS regime will have facilitated his recovery of £100,000 against A. But there is no reason why that regime should prevent B from recovering its costs out of the damages payable by A.***
>
> 25.***Any other result would give a claimant carte blanche to commence proceedings against as many defendants as he or she likes, requiring those defendants to run up large bills by way of costs, whilst remaining safe in the knowledge that, if the***

claim fails against all but one defendant, he or she will incur no costs liability of any kind to the successful defendants, despite the recovery of sums by way of damages from the unsuccessful defendant. That seems to me to be wrong in principle, because it would encourage the bringing of hopeless claims.

26. *The wording of the rule is consistent with that approach. There is nothing in r.44.14(1) which suggests that the claimant's fund (out of which the costs order will be met) is specific to the damages and interest payable by the defendant seeking to enforce the costs order, as opposed to the damages and interest payable by any other defendant. No such limitation can be discerned, and on the contrary, r.44.14(1) deals simply with orders for costs made against a claimant on the one hand, and orders for damages and interest made in favour of the claimant, on the other. The language is wide. It is clearly capable of embracing the situation in which defendant B has a claim for costs against the claimant which does not exceed the amount of the order for damages and interest made in favour of the claimant and payable by defendant A.*

Conclusions

It may be argued that if the majority of Portal Claims continue to exit the low value portal, and are litigated, these types of Claims are likely to remain profitable for Claimant Solicitors. As will be seen from later chapters, Employers' liability cases can be extremely complicated and the danger of using inexperienced fee earners can lead to matters being missed or claims with little or no prospects of success being progressed to litigation. The key to post-Jackson cases is arguably to identify 'winners' and 'losers' early on and that is what the remainder of this book will concentrate on.

CHAPTER THREE
EMPLOYERS' LIABILITY DISEASE ('ELD') CASES AND BASIC PRINCIPLES

Who is an employee?

Under ERA 1996, an "employee" is defined as an "*individual who has entered into or works under...a contract of employment*", and a "*contract of employment*" is defined, in turn, to mean "*a contract of service or apprenticeship, whether express or implied, and (if it is express) whether oral or in writing*". The 1996 Act sets out in full: -

> ***Statement of initial employment particulars.***
>
> *(1) Where an employee begins employment with an employer, the employer shall give to the employee a written statement of particulars of employment.*
>
> *(2) The statement may (subject to section 2(4)) be given in instalments and (whether or not given in instalments) shall be given not later than two months after the beginning of the employment.*
>
> *(3) The statement shall contain particulars of—*
>
> *(a) the names of the employer and employee,*
>
> *(b) the date when the employment began, and*
>
> *(c) the date on which the employee's period of continuous employment began (taking into account any employment with a previous employer which counts towards that period).*
>
> *(4) The statement shall also contain particulars, as at a specified date not more than seven days before the statement (or the instalment containing them) is given, of—*

(a) the scale or rate of remuneration or the method of calculating remuneration,

(b) the intervals at which remuneration is paid (that is, weekly, monthly or other specified intervals),

(c) any terms and conditions relating to hours of work (including any terms and conditions relating to normal working hours),

(d) any terms and conditions relating to any of the following—
(i) entitlement to holidays, including public holidays, and holiday pay (the particulars given being sufficient to enable the employee's entitlement, including any entitlement to accrued holiday pay on the termination of employment, to be precisely calculated),
(ii) incapacity for work due to sickness or injury, including any provision for sick pay, and
(iii) pensions and pension schemes,

(e) the length of notice which the employee is obliged to give and entitled to receive to terminate his contract of employment,

(f) the title of the job which the employee is employed to do or a brief description of the work for which he is employed,

(g) where the employment is not intended to be permanent, the period for which it is expected to continue or, if it is for a fixed term, the date when it is to end,

(h) either the place of work or, where the employee is required or permitted to work at various places, an indication of that and of the address of the employer,

(j) any collective agreements which directly affect the terms and conditions of the employment including, where the employer is not a party, the persons by whom they were made, and

(k) where the employee is required to work outside the United Kingdom for a period of more than one month—

> *(i) the period for which he is to work outside the United Kingdom,*
> *(ii) the currency in which remuneration is to be paid while he is working outside the United Kingdom,*
> *(iii) any additional remuneration payable to him, and any benefits to be provided to or in respect of him, by reason of his being required to work outside the United Kingdom, and*
> *(iv) any terms and conditions relating to his return to the United Kingdom.*

Parties to a contract will often, but not always, put the terms and conditions that govern the relationship into writing. There is no requirement for a contract of employment to be in writing, it can be written, oral or a mixture of both see *Dacas v Brook Street Bureau (UK) Limited [2004] IRLR.*

Lane v Shire Roofing Co (Oxford) Ltd [1995] *IRLR 493 : [1995] PIQR P417: Times, February 22, 1995* the Claimant was a building worker who was hired by the defendant employer to carry out a re-roofing job for which he was to be paid according to a daily rate. The defendant "*considered it prudent and advantageous to hire for individual jobs*". While carrying out the work, the Claimant fell and was injured. It was held that he was an employee for the purposes of the job, and so was owed the common law duty of care with regard to his health and safety. The Court found that the fact that he used his own tools or controlled his work were decisive but the question as to whose business he was engaged in had to be considered. The answer to that question depended on where the financial risk lay and whether and how far the workman had an opportunity of profiting from sound management in the performance of his task. Since the business which the plaintiff was engaged on was the defendants' business and not his own, the defendants owed the duties of employers to the plaintiff. The case is important as it looked a number of key cases which govern the employment relationship and the key passages from the Judgment are as follows in this context: -

> "*The next question is whether the respondents owed to the plaintiff the common law or statutory duty of an employer to his employees, or whether the appellant when doing that job was acting as an independent contractor. When it comes to the question of safety at work,*

there is a real public interest in recognising the employer/employee relationship when it exists, because of the responsibilities that the common law and statutes such as the Employers' Liability (Compulsory Insurance) Act 1969 places on the employer?

The judge was to find that the appellant was not an employee but was an independent contractor. In that event the appellant would have been responsible for his own safety; the respondent would have owed him no duty of care and would have had no responsibility (statutory or at common law) for the safety of the work done by the appellant.

We were taken through the standard authorities on this matter: ***Readymix Concrete (South East) Ltd. v. Minister of Pensions and National Insurance [1968] 2 QB 497; Market Investigations Ltd. v. Minister of Social Security [1969] 2 QB 173;*** *and Ferguson v. Dawson [1976] 1 WLR 1213, to name the principal ones. Two general remarks should be made. The overall employment background is very different today (and was, though less so, in 1986) than it had been at the time when those cases were decided. First, for a variety of reasons, there are more self-employed and fewer in employment. There is a greater flexibility in employment, with more temporary and shared employment. Second, there are perceived advantages for both workman and employer in the relationship between them being that of independent contractor. From the workman's point of view, being self-employed brings him into a more benevolent and less prompt taxation regime. From the employer's point of view, the protection of employee's rights contained in the employment protection legislation of the 1970s brought certain perceived disincentives to the employer to take on full-time long term employees. So even in 1986 there were reasons on both sides to avoid the employee label. But, as I have already said, there were, and are, good policy reasons in the safety at work field to ensure that the law properly categorises between employees and independent contractors.*

That line of authority shows that there are many factors to be taken into account in answering this question, and, with different

priority being given to those factors in different cases, all depends on the facts of each individual case.

Certain principles relevant to this case, however, emerge.

First, the element of control will be important: who lays down what is to be done, the way in which it is to be done, the means by which it is to be done, and the time when it is done?

Who provides (i.e. hires and fires) the team by which it is done, and who provides the material, plant and machinery and tools used?

But it is recognised that the control test may not be decisive *- for instance, in the case of skilled employees, with discretion to decide how their work should be done. In such cases the question is broadened to whose business was it: was the workman carrying on his own business, or was he carrying on that of his employers?* ***The American Supreme Court, in United States of America v. Silk (1946) 331 US 704,*** *asks the question whether the men were employees "as a matter of economic reality". The answer to this question may cover much of the same ground as the control test (such as whether he provides his own equipment and hires his own helpers)* ***but may involve looking to see where the financial risk lies, and whether and how far he has an opportunity of profiting from sound management in the performance of his task (see Market Investigations v. Minister of Social Security (supra at page 185).***

And these questions must be asked in the context of who is responsible for the overall safety of the men doing the work in question. *Mr.. Whittaker, of the respondents, was cross- examined on these lines, and he agreed that he was so responsible. Such an answer is not decisive (though it may be indicative) because ultimately the question is one of law, and he could be wrong as to where the legal responsibility lies".*

In summary, it therefore follows that the questions below are likely to establish whether an employer/employee relationship existed:-

1) Was there a written agreement or terms of employment?

2) If not, was there an oral agreement intended to create an employment relationship?

3) Did the employer have control of the premises where the accident took place?

4) Where did the financial risk lie, in other words, who profited from the task?

5) Who was responsible for the overall safety of the persons doing the work?

6) Who provided the materials, plant and machinery, and tools used in the role?

The Control Test – Further Authorities

Who had control of where the accident took place?

The case of *Performing Rights Society v Mitchell & Booker Ltd (1924) is of some assistance.* The defendants were sued for the breach of copyright by a jazz band. The defendant owned a dance-hall and had agreed in writing for a band to play at the hall as long as it did not infringe any copyright in the music it chose to perform. Unfortunately the band chose to play some music but did not have the plaintiff's permission. The plaintiff decided to sue the owners of the dance hall looking to hold them responsible for the actions of the band. However the defendant's liability depended on it being proved that the band were employed by them. The court looked at the facts that regular hours where worked each day by the band, there was a fixed period of employment, the band had been told where they should work, and they had exclusivity of service, there was also a right to dismiss the band for the breach of any fair instructions or requirement. In short the court looked at the 'nature and degree of detailed control over the person alleged to be a servant' and the band was held to be an employee. The

Court held that band members engaged to perform, were employees of the occupier of the dance hall as the agreement "*the right of continuous, dominant, and detailed control on every point, including the nature of the music to be played.*"

In *Gould v Minister of National Insurance (1951) 1 KB 731* at 734, stated "*The real question is one of the degrees of control exercised by the person employing...and this means not only the amount of control but the nature of that control and the direction in which it is exercised*"

In *Stevenson Jordan & Harrison Ltd v Macdonald and Evan [1952] 1 TLR 101* Denning LJ stated, "*...under a contract of service, a man is employed as part of the business, and his work is done as an integral part of the business; whereas under a contract for services his work, although done for the business is not integrated into it, but is only accessory to it...*".

The Common Law Duty of Care: A More Detailed Analysis

The common law duty of care is to take reasonable care to avoid injuring one's neighbours in accordance with *Donoghue v Stevenson [1932] AC 562.* Thus, an employer has a reasonable duty to take care for his employee's health and safety. It is contended that this calls for a reasonable response, taking into account the relationship of the parties, the magnitude of the risk of injury that was reasonable foreseeable, the seriousness of the consequences for the person for whom the risk is owed, the likelihood of the risk eventuating and the costs and practicality of preventing the risk (as in *Walker* below). In *Donoghue v Stevenson,* such a duty is primary and cannot be transferred to someone else, diluted, or delegated to employees.

In *Wilson & Clyde Co. Limited –v- English 1937 3 ALL ER 628*, Lord Wright said that the employer's duty is, "*personal to the employer to take reasonable care for the safety of his workmen, whether the employer be an individual, a firm or a company and whether or not the employer takes any share in the conduct of operations*".

Boyle v Kodak Limited [1969 1 WLR 661] is authority for the principle that, where a breach of statutory duty on the part of an employer has been proved, the claimant is entitled to some damages, even where he is also negligent, unless it can be shown that the employer's breach did not in fact contribute to the accident. Lord Reid cited the following passage from *Ginty v Belmont Building Supplies Ltd [at 666F]:*

> '***In my view, the important and fundamental question in a case like this is not whether there was a delegation, but simply the usual question: whose fault was it? If the answer to that question is that in substance and reality the accident was solely due to the fault of the plaintiff, so that he was the sole author of his own wrong, he is disentitled to recover.*** *But that has to be applied to the particular case and it is not necessarily conclusive for the employer to show that it was a wrongful act of the employee plaintiff which caused the accident. It might also appear from the evidence that something was done or omitted by the employer which caused or contributed to the accident: there may have been lack of proper supervision or lack of proper instructions; the employer may have employed for this purpose some insufficiently experienced men, or he may in the past have acquiesced in some wrong behaviour on the part of the men. Therefore, if one finds that the immediate and direct cause of the accident was some wrongful act of the man, that is not decisive.* ***One has to enquire whether the fault of the employer under the statutory regulations consists of, and is co-extensive with, the wrongful act of the employee. If there is some fault on the part of the employer which goes beyond or is independent of the wrongful act of the employee, and was the cause of the accident, the employer has some liability.***'

Safe Premises, Plant and Equipment

In *Latimer v AEC Limited [1953] AC643* the plaintiff was employed by the defendant. On the afternoon of the day of the accident, an exceptionally heavy rainstorm had flooded the whole of the defendant's premises. Oil, which normally ran in covered channels in the floor of the building, rose to the surface and when the water drained away, left an oily film on the floor. The defendants took measures to clean away the oil, using all the sawdust available to them. The plaintiff came on duty with the night shift, unaware of the condition of the floor. While endeavoring to place a heavy barrel on a trolley, his foot slipped on the still oily surface, he fell on his back, and the barrel crushed his left ankle. The trial judge found a breach of common law duty. The Court of Appeal reversed this decision. The Judgment in Latimer set out:-

> ***Lord Denning observed:"...in every case of foreseeable risk it is a matter of balancing the risk against the measures necessary to eliminate it."***

It is contended that the case of *Latimer* failed as the employer had taken some steps to eradicate the risk. This emphasizes that the law does not demand that the risk is eradicated entirely. If, in *Latimer*, no steps had been taken the outcome would have been entirely different. An employer therefore has a duty at common law to provide safe premises, plant and equipment but cannot be expected to eradicate risk entirely.

Safe System of Work

A useful illustration can be found in *Walker v Northumberland County Council [1995] IRLR 35.* The facts are outlined from the Judgment as follows:-

> *"The plaintiff worked for the defendants ("the Council") as an area social services officer from 1970 until December 1987. His position was one in middle management. He was responsible as manager for four teams of social services field workers in the Blyth Valley area of Northumberland. His office was at Cramlington. He in turn was answerable to the Assistant Director of the Field Services Division of the Council's Social Services Department. That was Mr. D N Davison. His office was at County Hall, Morpeth.Blyth Valley was one of five social service divisions in Northumberland. It was a pre-dominantly urban area and comprised a new town development at Cramlington with a relatively high proportion of young families with children many of whom had recently acquired houses which had pre-*

viously been local authority housing. It was an area which because of the social profile of the population was particularly productive of child-care problems falling within the ambit of responsibility of the Social Services Department. Amongst these problems in the course of the 1980s child abuse references were particularly prevalent. The population in Blyth Valley rose during this period and so did the volume of work which had to be undertaken by Mr. Walker and his teams of field workers. Although the number of field workers in the area had been increased during the period 1974 to 1978, there was no increase after 1978. By 1986 the pressure of work on those Social Service workers who were working in Blyth Valley had become very considerable. Not only were the teams of field workers under increased pressure, but so was Mr. Walker. The stress and anxiety created by that work pressure was intense. The increasing incidence of child abuse cases was particularly stressful for all concerned: for the field workers whose cases they were and who had to deal directly with the families and children and for Mr. Walker whose responsibility it was to make provision for the adequate manning of such cases by his teams of field social workers and for the holding of case conferences and the production of reports in respect of each child referred to the Department in his area of Blyth Valley.At the end of November 1986 Mr. Walker suffered a nervous breakdown. He suffered from mental exhaustion, acute anxiety, headaches, sleeplessness, irritability, inability to cope with any form of stress and a tendency to weep and to become upset. Under medical advice he remained off work until 4 March 1987. Mr. Walker was 50 on 10 March 1987.While off work Mr. Walker was treated by his family doctor and was seen by Dr D A Stephens, a very experienced psychiatrist who had known him professionally for many years by reason of Mr. Walker's social services work. Mr. Walker had no previous history of mental disorder and Dr Stephens observed that "his anxieties are sharply focused on work pressures, while a comprehensive review of all other areas of his life fail to produce any evidence of concurrent problems". He had known Mr. Walker "as a stable, industrious and committed colleague for many years and was surprised to hear about his recent difficulties".

The case is a good example of how the employer was liable at common law, for failing to provide a safe system of work. The key sections from the Judgment are:-

> "*The plaintiff's case is that the immediate superiors of Mr. Walker knew that social work is particularly stressful, that such stress can give rise to mental illness, that the workload falling upon Mr. Walker as area officer of the Blyth Valley area was by 1984 such as to impose increasing stress on Mr. Walker, that such workload became more stressful during the period 1984-1986 and that accordingly they ought reasonably to have foreseen that, unless they took steps to alleviate the impact of that workload, there was a real risk that Mr. Walker would suffer mental illness. In those circumstances, the Council's duty as employer of Mr. Walker being to take reasonable steps to provide a safe system of work, it was in breach of that duty in as much as the system of work was a threat to mental health which remained unremedied and caused Mr. Walker's mental breakdown.*
>
> *The Council's case is that, while it concedes that it owed to Mr. Walker a general duty to exercise reasonable care to provide him with a reasonably safe working system and to take reasonable steps to protect him from risks which are reasonably foreseeable, there was no breach of that duty: it was not reasonably foreseeable at any material time that Mr. Walker's work would impose upon him such stress as to give to a real risk of mental illness and alternatively, if such risk was reasonably foreseeable, the Council did not in all the circumstances, in particular, the budgetary constraints to which the Social Services Department was subject at the time, act unreasonably in failing to relieve the pressure on Mr. Walker. Mr. Simon Hawkesworth QC, on behalf of the Council has submitted that, in as much as the only effective remedial measures would have involved taking on more staff and therefore the allocation of additional funds for that purpose by the Social Services Department or, indeed the Council itself, and since the application of the Council's limited resources involved policymaking decisions as distinct from operational decisions, the Council cannot be said to have*

been in breach of any duty of care in having failed to take those decisions.

The Court looked at a number of helpful authorities with regards to foreseeability.

> ***"It is reasonably clear from the authorities that once a duty of care has been established the standard of care required for the performance of that duty must be measured against the yardstick of reasonable conduct on the part of a person in the position of that person who owes the duty. The law does not impose upon him the duty of an insurer against all injury or damage caused by him, however unlikely or unexpected and whatever the practical difficulties of guarding against it. It calls for no more than a reasonable response, what is reasonable being measured by the nature of the neighbourhood relationship, the magnitude of the risk of injury which was reasonably foreseeable, the seriousness of the consequence for the person to whom the duty is owed of the risk eventuating and the cost and practicability of preventing the risk.***
>
> *That these are the individual constituents of the yardstick of reasonable conduct is firmly supported by the observations of Lord Thankerton in Glasgow Corporation v Muir [1943] AC 448 at page 454:"In my opinion, it has long been held in Scotland that all that a person can be bound to foresee are the reasonable and probable consequences of the failure to take care, judged by the standard of the ordinary reasonable man....... The court must be careful to place itself in the position of the person charged with the duty and to consider what he or she should have reasonably anticipated as a natural and probable consequence of neglect, and not to give undue weight to the fact that a distressing accident has happened....."To the same effect is the speech of Lord Porter in Bolton v Stone, supra, at page 858:"* ***It is not enough that the event should be such as can reasonably be foreseen. The further result that injury is likely to follow must also be such as a reasonable man would contemplate before he can be convicted of actionable negligence. Nor is the remote possibility of injury occurring enough. There must be sufficient probability to lead a reasonable man to anticipate it. The existence of some risk***

> ***is an ordinary incident of life, even when all due care has been, as it must be, taken.*** *"And in Paris v Stepney Borough Council [1951] AC 367 at page 375 Lord Simonds expressly recognised the potential seriousness of injury as a relevant factor in assessing the standard of care to be expected of the reasonable employer. In Latimer v AEC Ltd [1952] 2 QB 701, Lord Denning observed: "...in every case of foreseeable risk it is a matter of balancing the risk against the measures necessary to eliminate it."and in* ***Overseas Tankship (UK) Ltd v The Miller Steamship Co Ltd [1967] AC 617 at page 542, Lord Reid said:"It does not follow that, no matter what the circumstances may be, it is justifiable to neglect a risk of such a small magnitude. A reasonable man would only neglect such a risk if he had some valid reason for doing so, eg that it would involve considerable expense to eliminate the risk. He would weigh the risk against the difficulty of eliminating it."The practicability of remedial measures must clearly take into account the resources and facilities at the disposal of the person or body owing the duty of care:*** *see Lord Reid in British Railways Board v Herrington [1972] AC 877 at page 899, and the purpose of the activity which has given rise to the risk of injury: the risk must be balanced "against the end to be achieved": see Denning LJ in Watt v Hertfordshire CC [1954] 1 WLR 835 at page 838. of harm".*

In *Walker*, the Court concluded, finding the Defendant liable:-

> "***That said, the duty of an employer public body, whether in contract or tort, to provide a safe system of work is, as I have said, a duty only to do what is reasonable,*** *and in many cases it may be necessary to take into account decisions which are within the policy-making area and the reasons for those decisions in order to test whether the body's conduct has been reasonable. In that exercise there can be no basis for treating the public body differently in principle from any other commercial employer, although there would have to be taken into account considerations such as budgetary constraints and perhaps lack of flexibility of decision-taking which might not arise with a commercial employer.Having regard to the reasonably foreseeable size of the risk of repetition of Mr. Walker's illness if his duties were not alleviated by effective additional assistance and to the*

reasonably foreseeable gravity of the mental breakdown which might result if nothing were done, I have come to the conclusion that the standard of care to be expected of a reasonable local authority required that in March 1987 such additional assistance should be provided if not on a permanent basis, at least until restructuring of the Social Services had been effected and the workload on Mr. Walker thereby permanently reduced. That measure of additional assistance ought to have been provided notwithstanding that it could be expected to have some disruptive effect on the Council's provision of services to the public. ***When Mr. Walker returned from his first illness the Council had to decide whether it was prepared to go on employing him in spite of the fact that he had made it sufficiently clear that he must have effective additional help if he was to continue at Blyth Valley. It chose to continue to employ him, but provided no effective help. In so doing it was, in my judgment, acting unreasonably and therefore in breach of its duty of care.I understand it to be accepted that if there was breach of duty damage was caused by that breach. However, in view of the fact that I have decided this case on the second breakdown alone, it is right to add that I am satisfied on the evidence that had the further assistance been provided to Mr. Walker, his second breakdown would probably not have occurred.In the event, there will be judgment for the plaintiff on liability with damages yet to be assessed".***

Health and Safety at Work Act 1974 Further Information

Breach of the Regulations under the 1974 Act does not in itself afford a cause of action. The Act sets out: -

2 - General duties of employers to their employees.

(1) It shall be the duty of every employer to ensure, so far as is reasonably practicable, the health, safety and welfare at work of all his employees.

(2) Without prejudice to the generality of an employer's duty under the preceding subsection, the matters to which that duty extends include in particular—

(a) the provision and maintenance of plant and systems of work that are, so far as is reasonably practicable, safe and without risks to health;

(b) arrangements for ensuring, so far as is reasonably practicable, safety and absence of risks to health in connection with the use, handling, storage and transport of articles and substances;

(c) the provision of such information, instruction, training and supervision as is necessary to ensure, , the health and safety at work of his employees;

(d) so far as is reasonably practicable as regards any place of work under the employer's control, the maintenance of it in a condition that is safe and without risks to health and the provision and maintenance of means of access to and egress from it that are safe and without such risks;

(e) the provision and maintenance of a working environment for his employees that is, so far as is reasonably practicable, safe, without risks to health, and adequate as regards facilities and arrangements for their welfare at work.

(3) Except in such cases as may be prescribed, it shall be the duty of every employer to prepare and as often as may be appropriate revise a written statement of his general policy with respect to the health and safety at work of his employees and the organisation and arrangements for the time being in force for carrying out that policy, and to bring the statement and any revision of it to the notice of all of his employees.

The burden of proving that compliance with an obligation was not 'reasonably practical' is on the Defendant as per section 40 which sets out:-

40

Onus of proving limits of what is practicable etc.

In any proceedings for an offence under any of the relevant statutory provisions consisting of a failure to comply with a duty or requirement to do something so far as is practicable or so far as is reasonably practicable, or to use the best practicable means to do something, it shall be for the accused to prove (as the case may be) that it was not practicable or not reasonably practicable to do more than was in fact done to satisfy the duty or requirement, or that there was no better practicable means than was in fact used to satisfy the duty or requirement.

By section 15 of the Regulations, the Secretary of State has the power to make Health and Safety Regulations. Breach of the Regulations gives rise to civil liability (for accidents before October 2013 as set out in the ERRA Chapter), unless the Regulations states otherwise (see section 74).

Self Employed Individuals and Agency Workers

Difficulties can sometimes arise in the context of self-employed workers and agency workers as to who had the duty of care in such circumstances.

In the case of agency workers, sometimes, a worker will be employed by an agency and be sent to work at the site of the client. In these circumstances the case of *ROBERT PAUL BAILEY V (1) COMMAND SECURITY SERVICES LTD (2) TJX INC (USA) (A FIRM) (2001), where Liability was established and apportioned between the employer of the claimant and the owner of the warehouse in which he was injured when he fell down an unguarded lift shaft.* In the instant case the first defendant, the employer, had failed to carry out a risk assessment of the warehouse, where a security guard had sustained injury. The First Defendant had never visited the premises of the client. In order words *Bailey*, indicates that an agency may be liable to some extent, if its risk assessments were inadequate, and it had not carried out a site survey, before sending the claimant to work there, which in this case, may have revealed the lack of safety equipment, in my view. The Court said that the first defendant owed no duty under Regulation13 of the Regulations because the accident site was not under its control at the relevant time. However, the first defendant was negligent in that it did not carry out any thorough risk assessment of the premises. If it had have carried out a risk assessment, it would have recognised that the unguarded lift shaft posed a danger to its employees.

A similar problem sometimes arises in the context of self-employed contractors, for example, those working on building sites. Whilst sub-contractors are responsible for their own safety, if the main occupier/contractor is negligent in providing a safe workplace or site location, the main contractor may be liable for an accident at work claim. In this context the control test becomes important, and whether the contractor was working on a site controlled by a third party and/ or under the direction of a third party gains significance. The reader is referred to the control section of this chapter in this context. Section 3 of the Health and Safety at Work Act 1974 sets out as follows:-

> ***General duties of employers and self-employed to persons other than their employees.***
>
> *(1) It shall be the duty of every employer to conduct his undertaking in such a way as to ensure, so far as is reasonably practicable, that persons not in his employment who may be affected thereby are not thereby exposed to risks to their health or safety.*
>
> *(2) It shall be the duty of every self-employed person to conduct his undertaking in such a way as to ensure, so far as is reasonably practicable, that he and other persons (not being his employees) who may be affected thereby are not thereby exposed to risks to their health or safety.*
>
> *(3) In such cases as may be prescribed, it shall be the duty of every employer and every self-employed person, in the prescribed circumstances and in the prescribed manner, to give to persons (not being his*

employees) who may be affected by the way in which he conducts his undertaking the prescribed information about such aspects of the way in which he conducts his undertaking as might affect their health or safety.

In *R v Associated Octel Co Limited [1997]*, the Court looked at the liability of independent contractors and found the employer was liable in this instance. RGP Ltd was convicted of an offence under section 2 of the 1974 Act, and Octel Ltd of an offence under section 3. Octel Ltd appealed to the Court of Appeal. It was argued on their behalf that section 3 did not involve liability for the actions of independent contractors.

The court ruled that it was a question of fact in each case, as to whether an activity, which caused risk to the health and safety of persons (other than employees), amounted to the conduct of an undertaking. The term "undertaking" was taken as meaning "enterprise" or "business" and the cleaning, maintenance or repair of plant, machinery or buildings necessary for carrying on the business was part of the undertaking (whether carried out by the client's employees or by an independent contractor). Therefore, Octel Ltd was liable under section 3(1).

Contributory Negligence

Section 7 of the Health and Safety at Work 1974 sets out:-

7

General duties of employees at work.

It shall be the duty of every employee while at work—

(a) ***to take reasonable care for the health and safety of himself and of other persons who may be affected by his acts or omissions at work; and***

> *(b) as regards any duty or requirement imposed on his employer or any other person by or under any of the relevant statutory provisions, to co-operate with him so far as is necessary to enable that duty or requirement to be performed or complied with.*

In *Jones –v- Lovox Quarries Limited 1952 2QB 608,* Denning LJ said "*a person is guilty of contributory negligence if you ought reasonably to have foreseen that if he did not act as a reasonable, prudent man, he might hurt himself, and in his reckonings he must take into account the possibility of others being careless. If a man carelessly rides on a vehicle in a dangerous position and subsequently there is a collision in which his injuries are made worse by reason of his position than they would otherwise have been, then his damage is partly the result of his own fault and the damages recoverable by him to be reduced accordingly. In my opinion, even if the Court was to find primary liability on behalf of the First Defendant, in respect of the issues regarding lack of training records and risk assessments, in my opinion there is a potential for up to 50% contributory negligence on behalf of the Claimant for the reasons set out above*".

In *Anderson v Newham College of Further Education [2003] ICR 212,* the Judge found that the Defendant employers were in breach of statutory duty under Regulation 12(3) of the Workplace (Health, Safety and Welfare) Regulations 1992, because a white-board in a classroom was stored in a dangerous position, so as to create a tripping hazard. The judge also held that the claimant employee was contributorily negligent in failing to see and avoid the hazard and reduced his damages by 90%. The Court of Appeal held that:

> '***Whether a claim was in negligence or breach of statutory duty, if the evidence showed the entire fault to lie with the claimant, there was no liability on the defendant and section 1(1) of the Law Reform (Contributory Negligence) Act 1945 did not bite: if there was liability, contributory negligence could reduce its monetary quantification under section 1(1) but could not legally or logically nullify it; but that a high standard of proof was required to shift the entire blame for a breach of statutory duty from an employer to an injured employee...and that the fair apportionment of liability by reason of contributory negligence was 50%***'

Thus, it is always necessary to consider the issue of contributory negligence in any claim. For example:

a) Did the claimant know the act he was undertaking was dangerous?

b) If the claimant was trained, or was in a senior position, should he have known the Act he was undertaking was dangerous?

Conclusions

As can be seen, the law in this area is extremely complex, and this chapter is designed to provide the reader with the basics, and a range of cases that can assist as a starting point to an investigation. The remaining chapters will discuss the Regulations and investigating various types of accidents at work in more detail, including, establishing liability.

CHAPTER FOUR
TIPS FOR EARLY INVESTIGATIONS

It is clear that in Employers' Liability matters, post-Jackson and post-31st July 2013, the incentives for defendants and insurers to settle these cases, has now been substantially reduced. These cases are now subject to portal and fixed recoverable costs, and as we have seen from previous chapters, the insurer can now run three or four of these claims to trial and lose them, for effectively the same costs as running one CFA claim to trial, with a 100% uplift under the pre-Jackson regime and losing that claim at trial.

This new litigation landscape of course, poses enormous difficulties for claimant lawyers. The '50/50' cases that previously may have been issued and settled, before trial, are arguably less likely to occur. This means that law firms, more than ever, will have to be very careful to vet claims before taking them on. To run a profitable department post-Jackson, the majority of claims incepted will have to succeed, given there is no longer the flexibility of CFA uplifts to cushion the shortfalls of the cases that are lost at trial.

This chapter deals with utilising the new amendments to the CPR post April 2013 and post July 2013, when the Jackson reforms came into effect to:

a) Vet cases early on;
b) Obtain disclosure quickly; and
c) Encourage settlement pre-trial, using Part 36 to do that.

Pre-Action Protocols

If a case exits the Low Value Portal, i.e. because liability has been denied or liability has not been admitted by the defendant (or for any other reason), then the case will still fall within the personal injury pre action protocol, which states as follows: -

"3.7

The Defendant will have a ***maximum of three months*** *from the date of acknowledgment of the claim* ***to investigate****. No later than the end of that period the defendant (insurer) shall reply, stating whether liability is denied and, if so, giving reasons for their denial of liability including any alternative version of events relied upon"*

Further, it goes on:-

"3.10

If the ***defendant denies liability****, he should enclose with the letter of reply,* ***documents*** *in his possession which are* ***material to the issues*** *between the parties, and which would be likely to be ordered to be disclosed by the court, either on an application for pre-action disclosure, or on disclosure during proceedings.*

3.11

Attached at Annex B are ***specimen****, but non-exhaustive,* ***lists*** *of documents likely to be material in different types of claims. Where the claimant's investigation of the case is well advanced, the letter of claim could indicate which classes of documents are considered relevant for early disclosure. Alternatively, these could be identified at a later stage.*

3.12

Where the defendant admits primary liability, but alleges contributory negligence by the claimant, the defendant should give reasons supporting those allegations and disclose those documents from Annex B which are relevant to the issues in dispute. The claimant should respond to the allegations of contributory negligence before proceedings are issued".

Pre-Action Protocols – Employers' Liability Claims

The Pre-Action Protocol for Employers' liability Claims, suggests the following disclosure should be provided by the Defendant, once the claim has fallen out of the Portal. The type of disclosure will depend upon the facts, however, the following is contained within the Protocol:-

WORKPLACE CLAIMS - GENERAL DOCUMENTS

a) accident book entry;
b) other entries in the book or other accident books, relating to accidents or injuries similar to those suffered by our client (and if it is contended there are no such entries please confirm we may have facilities to inspect all accident books);
c) first aider report;
d) surgery record;
e) foreman/supervisor accident report;
f) safety representative's accident report;
g) RIDDOR (Reporting of Injuries, Diseases and Dangerous Occurrences Regulations) reported to HSE or relevant investigatory agency;
h) back to work interview notes and report;
i) all personnel/occupational health records relating to our client;
j) other communications between defendants and HSE or other relevant
k) investigatory agency;
l) minutes of Health and Safety Committee meeting(s) where accident/matter
m) considered;
n) copies of all relevant CCTV footage and any other relevant photographs, videos and/or DVDs;
o) copies of all electronic communications/documentation relating to the accident;
p) earnings information where defendant is employer;
q) reports to DWP;
r) manufacturer's or dealers instructions or recommendations concerning use of
s) the work equipment;

t) service or maintenance records of the work equipment;
u) all documents recording arrangements for detecting, removing or cleaning up any articles or substances on the floor of the premises likely to cause a trip or slip;
v) work sheets and all other documents completed by or on behalf of those
w) responsible for implementing the cleaning policy and recording work done;
x) all invoices, receipts and other documents relating to the purchase of relevant
y) safety equipment to prevent a repetition of the accident;
z) all correspondence, memoranda or other documentation received or brought
aa) into being concerning the condition or repair of the work equipment/the premises;
bb) all correspondence, instructions, estimates, invoices and other documentation submitted or received concerning repairs, remedial works or other works to the work equipment/the premises since the date of that accident;
cc) work sheets and all other documents recording work done completed by those responsible for maintaining the work equipment/premises;
dd) all relevant risk assessments;
ee) all reports, conclusions or recommendations following any enquiry or investigation into the accident;
ff) the record kept of complaints made by employees together with all other documents recording in any way such complaints or actions taken thereon;
gg) all other correspondence sent, or received, relating to our client's injury prior to receipt of this letter of claim;
hh) documents listed above relating to any previous/similar accident/matter
ii) identified by the claimant and relied upon as proof of negligence including accident
jj) book entries;

WORKPLACE CLAIMS – DISCLOSURE WHERE SPECIFIC REGULATIONS APPLY.

SECTION A –

Management of Health and Safety at Work Regulations 1999

Documents including—

a) Pre-accident Risk Assessment required by Regulation 3(1);
b) Post-accident Re-Assessment required by Regulation 3(2);
c) Accident Investigation Report prepared in implementing the requirements of
d) Regulations 4, and 5;
e) Health Surveillance Records in appropriate cases required by Regulation 6;
f) documents relating to the appointment of competent persons to assist required by Regulation 7;
g) documents relating to the employees health and safety training required by
h) Regulation 8;
i) documents relating to necessary contacts with external services required by
j) Regulation 9;
k) information provided to employees under Regulation 10.

SECTION B–

Workplace (Health Safety and Welfare) Regulations 1992

Documents including—

a) repair and maintenance records required by Regulation 5;
b) housekeeping records to comply with the requirements of Regulation 9;
c) hazard warning signs or notices to comply with Regulation 17 (Traffic Routes).

SECTION C –

Provision and Use of Work Equipment Regulations 1998

Documents including—

a) manufacturers' specifications and instructions in respect of relevant work
b) equipment establishing its suitability to comply with Regulation 4;
c) maintenance log/maintenance records required to comply with Regulation 5;
d) documents providing information and instructions to employees to comply with
e) Regulation 8;
f) documents provided to the employee in respect of training for use to comply with Regulation 9;
g) risk assessments/documents required to comply with Regulation 12;
h) any notice, sign or document relied upon as a defence to alleged breaches of
i) Regulations 14 to 18 dealing with controls and control systems;
j) instruction/training documents issued to comply with the requirements of
k) Regulation 22 insofar as it deals with maintenance operations where the machinery
l) is not shut down;
m) copies of markings required to comply with Regulation 23;
n) copies of warnings required to comply with Regulation 24.

SECTION D –

Personal Protective Equipment at Work Regulations 1992

Documents including—

a) documents relating to the assessment of the Personal Protective Equipment to
b) comply with Regulation 6;

c) documents relating to the maintenance and replacement of Personal Protective
d) Equipment to comply with Regulation 7;
e) record of maintenance procedures for Personal Protective Equipment to comply
f) with Regulation 7;
g) records of tests and examinations of Personal Protective Equipment to comply
h) with Regulation 7;
i) documents providing information, instruction and training in relation to the
j) Personal Protective Equipment to comply with Regulation 9;
k) instructions for use of Personal Protective Equipment to include the manufacturers' instructions to comply with Regulation 10.

SECTION E –

Manual Handling Operations Regulations 1992

Documents including—

a) Manual Handling Risk Assessment carried out to comply with the requirements of Regulation 4(1)(b)(i);
b) re-assessment carried out post-accident to comply with requirements of
c) Regulation 4(1)(b)(i);
d) documents showing the information provided to the employee to give general
e) indications related to the load and precise indications on the weight of the load and
f) the heaviest side of the load if the centre of gravity was not positioned centrally to
g) comply with Regulation 4(1)(b)(iii);
h) documents relating to training in respect of manual handling operations and
i) training records.

SECTION F –

Health and Safety (Display Screen Equipment) Regulations 1992

Documents including—

a) analysis of work stations to assess and reduce risks carried out to comply with the requirements of Regulation 2;

b) re-assessment of analysis of work stations to assess and reduce risks following

c) development of symptoms by the claimant;

d) documents detailing the provision of training including training records to comply with the requirements of Regulation 6;

e) documents providing information to employees to comply with the requirements of Regulation 7.

SECTION H –

Construction (Design and Management) Regulations 2007

Documents including—

a) notification of a project form (HSE F10) to comply with the requirements of
b) Regulation 7;
c) Health and Safety Plan to comply with requirements of Regulation 15;
d) Health and Safety file to comply with the requirements of Regulations 12 and 14;
e) information and training records provided to comply with the requirements of
f) Regulation 17;
g) records of advice from and views of persons at work to comply with the

h) requirements of Regulation 18;
i) reports of inspections made in accordance with Regulation 33;
j) records of checks for the purposes of Regulation 34;
k) emergency procedures for the purposes of Regulation 39.

SECTION I –

Construction (Health, Safety & Welfare) Regulations 1996

Documents including—

a) documents produced to comply with requirements of the Regulations.

SECTION J –

Work at Height Regulations 2005

Documents including—

a) documents relating to planning, supervision and safety carried out for Regulation 4;
b) documents relating to training for the purposes of Regulation 5;
c) documents relating to the risk assessment carried out for Regulation 6;
d) documents relating to the selection of work equipment for the purposes of
e) Regulation 7;
f) notices or other means in writing warning of fragile surfaces for the purposes of
g) Regulation 9;
h) documents relating to any inspection carried out for Regulation 12;
i) documents relating to any inspection carried out for Regulation 13;
j) reports made for the purposes of Regulation 14;
k) any certificate issued for the purposes of Regulation 15.

It is advisable that the letter requesting the disclosure is sent to the Defendant or their representatives, as soon as the case exits the portal.

Following that letter, a further request is made 14 days before the end of the protocol period and a final request at the end of the protocol period. Each request should say that if the *full* documentation is not disclosed, an Application will be made for Pre-Action Disclosure at the end of the protocol period, and the costs sought of the application, without any further recourse or warning. This will give the defendant plenty of notice of the application and should give the claimant some chance of recovering the costs of the application at the hearing. It should be borne in mind that on an Application for Pre-Action Disclosure, the general rule is that the party making the disclosure gets the costs of the application unless there has been some unreasonable conduct in responding to the disclosure requests. This is why these letters are important, in terms of displacing this general rule and seeking the costs of the application.

As an additional point, should the defendant says it does not hold a document, it should be asked to sign a disclosure statement, with an appropriate statement of truth, to say the document is not available.

Applications for Pre-Action Disclosure

It is arguable that pre-action disclosure applications are one of the most common applications in personal injury litigation. Unlike a road traffic claim, the defendant's disclosure is almost always required to assess a potential defence in an employer's liability claim.

The CPR sets out:-

Disclosure before proceedings start

> "*31.16*
>
> *(1) This rule applies where an application is made to the court under any Act for disclosure before proceedings have started1.*
>
> *(2) The application must be supported by evidence.*

(3) The court may make an order under this rule only where:-
(a) the respondent is likely to be a party to subsequent proceedings;
(b) the applicant is also likely to be a party to those proceedings;
(c) if proceedings have started, the respondent's duty by way of standard disclosure, set out in rule 31.6, would extend to the documents or classes of documents of which the applicant seeks disclosure; and
(d) disclosure before proceedings have started is desirable in order to:-
(i) dispose fairly of the anticipated proceedings;
(ii) assist the dispute to be resolved without proceedings; or
(iii) save costs.

(4) An order under this rule must:-
(a) specify the documents or the classes of documents which the respondent must disclose; and
(b) require him, when making disclosure, to specify any of those documents:-
(i) which are no longer in his control; or
(ii) in respect of which he claims a right or duty to withhold inspection.

(5) Such an order may:-
(a) require the respondent to indicate what has happened to any documents which are no longer in his control; and
(b) specify the time and place for disclosure and inspection".

It is arguable that as soon as the case reaches the end of the protocol period, if full disclosure has not been provided to enable the claimant's lawyer to assess the claim, an application should be made, having followed the process above given that:

a) the claimant's lawyer within fixed costs needs the documents to assess the prospects of success;
b) a decision cannot be reached without those documents; and
c) the pre-action protocols (in most scenarios) are very specific as to what should be disclosed pre-issue.

In making the application it is important that the application sets out in detail:

a) what the accident circumstances are;
b) the nature of the claimant's investigations;
c) what response the defendant has made to the request; and
d) most importantly, why each of the documents are required.

The majority of PAD applications, in the author's experience, settle before they ever get to a hearing, but it is clear post-Jackson, it is more important than ever that disclosure is given in full and on time, to enable claimant lawyers to make quick and efficient decisions, about which cases are to be closed and which are to be litigated. It must be the case, that with Fixed Recoverable Costs, it will no longer be efficient to chase defendants for documents for months or even years, whilst cases, which are likely to have less than 50% prospects, are sat in claimant lawyers' cabinets waiting for disclosure to come in order to assess them.

Part 36 – Making the Defendant Settle, Once Out of The Low Value Portal For Post 31 July 2013 Cases

Post-Jackson, one of the only ways that the Defendant may be encouraged to settle an employers' liability case, or any other claim for that matter, which stays within fixed costs, may be by the updated Part 36 rules, which came into effect in July 2013. These updates are as set out as follows:-

> *36.14 - Costs consequences following judgment- Trial / Disposal*
>
> *(1) Subject to rule 36.14A, **this rule applies whereupon judgment being entered:-***
> ***(b) judgment against the defendant is at least as advantageous to the claimant as the proposals contained in a claimant's Part 36 offer.***
>
> *(1A) For the purposes of paragraph (1), in relation to any money claim or money element of a claim, '**more advantageous**' means*

better in money terms by any amount, however small, and 'at least as advantageous' shall be construed accordingly.

(3) Subject to paragraph (6), where rule 36.14(1)(b) applies, the court will, unless it considers it unjust to do so, order that the claimant is entitled to –
(a) interest on the whole or part of any sum of money (excluding interest) awarded at a rate not exceeding 10% above base rate(GL) for some or all of the period starting with the date on which the relevant period expired;
(b) his costs on the indemnity basis from the date on which the relevant period expired;
(c) interest on those costs at a rate not exceeding 10% above base rate(GL); and
(d) an additional amount, which shall not exceed £75,000, calculated by applying the prescribed percentage set out below to an amount which is –
(ii) where the claim is only a non-monetary claim, the sum awarded to the claimant by the court in respect of costs –

It is arguable that early Part 36 offers on Employers' Liability Cases cases are essential, as this is now the only way defendants will be encouraged to settle claims, as the costs consequences for the defendant are severe, if the claimant beats its own Part 36 offer at trial. It may be advisable therefore that a realistic Part 36 offer should be made as soon as possible, and as soon as possible after directions have been given and the claim has been allocated to track. The Claimant should remember however that if the case is allocated to the multi-track, fixed recoverable costs will not apply.

It is important that the Part 36 offer is a realistic one, rather than as a starting point of negotiations, the earlier the Part 36 offer is made, the greater the consequences for the defendant, if the offer is not beaten at Trial, and thus the more weight the defendant is likely to give to that offer when considering whether to accept it or not.

Defendant Part 36 Rules In Post July 2013 FRC Cases

It is still the reality that for cases that stay allocated to the fast track, and thus within fixed recoverable costs, any Part 36 offers made by the Defendant will still apply and thus still 'bite'. It therefore may remain prudent for the claimant to obtain ATE cover in any event, to insure against that risk.

36.14 - Costs consequences following judgment

(1) Subject to rule 36.14A, this rule applies whereupon judgment being entered:-
(a) a claimant fails to obtain a judgment more advantageous than a defendant's Part 36 offer; *or*

(1A) For the purposes of paragraph (1), in relation to any money claim or money element of a claim, 'more advantageous' means better in money terms by any amount, however small, and 'at least as advantageous' shall be construed accordingly.

(2) Subject to paragraph (6), where rule 36.14(1)(a) applies, the court will, unless it considers it unjust to do so, order that the defendant is entitled to:-
(a) his costs from the date on which the relevant period expired; and
(b) interest on those costs.

45.29F - Defendants' costs

(1) In this rule:-
(a) paragraphs (8) and (9) apply to assessments of defendants' costs under Part 36;

2) If, in any case to which this Section applies, the court makes an order for costs in favour of the defendant:-
(a) the court will have regard to; and
(b) the amount of costs ordered to be paid shall not exceed,

the amount which would have been payable by the defendant if an order for costs had been made in favour of the claimant at the same stage of the proceedings.

(3) For the purpose of assessing the costs payable to the defendant by reference to the fixed costs in Table 6, Table 6A, Table 6B, Table 6C and Table 6D, "value of the claim for damages" and "damages" shall be treated as references to the value of the claim.

In other words, if the claimant fails to obtain a judgment more advantageous than a defendant's Part 36 offer, then, unless the court considers it unjust, the claimant gets the fixed costs under the relevant table up to the stage the case had reached at the end of the relevant period, but must pay the defendant's costs from the end of the relevant period, to the date of judgment, subject to capping.

Where a defendant is awarded costs, the maximum amount of costs payable by the claimant to the defendant is the difference between the fixed costs applicable at the date of acceptance less the costs to which the claimant is entitled.

Allocation Post-July 2013 cases

Following on from the above, it may be argued that allocation will become the new battleground between claimants and defendants. Claimants will want the case allocated to the multi-track, to escape fixed recoverable costs, and defendants will want the case allocated to the fast track to keep within fixed recoverable costs. The difficulty for claimants is that the Court is likely to view the majority of employers' liability cases as relatively straight forward matters that can be dealt with in the fast track but CPR 26.8 sets out:-

26.8 - Matters relevant to allocation to a track

(1) When deciding the track for a claim, the matters to which the court shall have regard include:-
(a) the financial value, if any, of the claim;

(b) the nature of the remedy sought;
(c) the likely complexity of the facts, law or evidence;
(d) the number of parties or likely parties;
(e) the value of any counterclaim or other Part 20 claim and the complexity of any matters relating to it;
(f) the amount of oral evidence which may be required;
(g) the importance of the claim to persons who are not parties to the proceedings;
(h) the views expressed by the parties; and
(i) the circumstances of the parties.

Given that the court in most cases now allocates initially on paper to a track, it may be a good idea that if, for a claimant, is:

a) complex in law; or
b) complex in fact; or
c) requires numerous experts; or
d) is likely to require oral expert evidence; or
e) is going to last more than 1 day due to the number of witnesses

the claimant drafts submissions and returns these to the court, with the directions questionnaire and asks for the matter to be listed for a CMC, to determine the issue of track, should the claimant wants the claim to be allocated to the multi-track. The general rule is that if the case is likely to last more than 1 day, it needs to be allocated to the multi-track. It may be advisable that if the case is likely to last more than 1 day, a draft trial timetable is submitted to the court, setting out why and how, to support the Claimant's submissions in this regard.

Many more complex employers' liability cases, particularly where there may be multiple defendants, more serious injuries, or, where there are complex disputes of fact, should be allocated to the multi-track, to allow for provision of expert evidence on both fact and causation, if required. However, whichever track a matter is allocated to, and even if it remains within fixed recoverable costs, a claimant lawyer still of course has a duty to obtain all appropriate evidence to support the case and investigate to the fullest extent, even if it remains within the fixed recoverable cost scheme. It may well be that defendants are prepared to sacrifice their own medical expert, to keep cases out of the multi-track and in fixed recoverable costs. This will of course be of interest in the way of future developments.

Summary

It seems clear that there are a number of tactical decisions to be made early on in employers' liability cases post-Jackson, and, in particular, issues surrounding allocation of track, when to make a Part 36 offer and when to make applications for disclosure. However, if one makes astute tactical decisions, these course of action will allow this type of work to remain economical for claimant law firms and thereafter, permit claimants, continued access to justice.

CHAPTER FIVE
THE ENTERPRISE AND REGULATORY REFORM ACT 2013

Section 69 of the Enterprise and Regulatory Reform Act 2013 ('ERRA 2013') is now in force. The effect of Section 69 is that most employees, seeking compensation for injuries suffered as a result of accidents at work on or after 1 October 2013, will no longer be able solely to rely on a breach of health and safety regulations to establish breach of duty. Instead, they will only be able to seek compensation where it can be shown that the employer breached the common law duty of care.

Under the 'Six Pack' Regulations which came into place in 1992, to allow the UK to comply with various European Directives, the employer could find themselves liable, for example, for defective work equipment, even where it had been maintained and inspected properly. The aim of the legislation is to remove the time and cost of the burden of complying with the Regulations from employers. This will however, in turn, make it more difficult for Claimants to succeed in EL claims.

Section 69 of the ERRA 2013 sets out as follows:-

Civil liability for breach of health and safety duties

(1) Section 47 of the Health and Safety at Work etc. Act 1974 (civil liability) is amended as set out in subsections (2) to (7).

(2) In subsection (1), omit paragraph (b) (including the "or" at the end of that paragraph).

(3) For subsection (2) substitute—
"(2) Breach of a duty imposed by a statutory instrument containing (whether alone or with other provision) health and safety regulations shall not be actionable except to the extent that regulations under this section so provide.

(2A) Breach of a duty imposed by an existing statutory provision shall not be actionable except to the extent that regulations under this section so provide (including by modifying any of the existing statutory provisions).

(2B) Regulations under this section may include provision for—
(a) a defence to be available in any action for breach of the duty mentioned in subsection (2) or (2A);
(b) any term of an agreement which purports to exclude or restrict any liability for such a breach to be void."

(4) In subsection (3), omit the words from ", whether brought by virtue of subsection (2)" to the end.

(5) In subsection (4)—
(a) for "and (2)" substitute " , (2) and (2A) ", and
(b) for "(3)" substitute " (2B)(a) ".

(6) Omit subsections (5) and (6).

(7) After subsection (6) insert—
"(7) The power to make regulations under this section shall be exercisable by the Secretary of State."

(8) Where, on the commencement of this section, there is in force an Order in Council made under section 84(3) of the Health and Safety at Work etc. Act 1974 that applies to matters outside Great Britain any of the provisions of that Act that are amended by this section, that Order is to be taken as applying those provisions as so amended.

(9) The amendments made by this section do not apply in relation to breach of a duty which it would be within the legislative competence of the Scottish Parliament to impose by an Act of that Parliament.

(10) The amendments made by this section do not apply in relation to breach of a duty where that breach occurs before the commencement of this section.

The explanatory notes to the ERRA also state: "*The amendment... reverses the present position on civil liability, with the effect, unless any exceptions apply, that it will only be possible to claim for compensation in relation to affected health and safety legislation where it can be proved that the duty holder (usually the employer) has been negligent. This means that in future, for all relevant claims, duty-holders will only have to defend themselves against negligence.*"

A Historical Perspective

In order to look at the impact upon Employers' Liability Claims, it is necessary to look at matters from a historical perspective. The new Regulations make changes to Sections 15 and 47 (2) of the *Health and Safety at Work Act 1974* which sets out:-

> *15*
>
> ***Health and safety regulations.***
>
> *[**F34**(1) Subject to the provisions of section 50, the Secretary of State **F35**. . . shall have power to make regulations under this section for any of the general purposes of this Part (and regulations so made are in this Part referred to as "health and safety regulations").]*
>
> *(2) Without prejudice to the generality of the preceding subsection, health and safety regulations may for any of the general purposes of this Part make provision for any of the purposes mentioned in Schedule 3.*
>
> *(3) Health and safety regulations—*
> *(a) may repeal or modify any of the existing statutory provisions;*
> *(b) may exclude or modify in relation to any specified class of case any of the provisions of sections 2 to 9 or any of the existing statutory provisions;*
> *(c) may make a specified authority or class of authorities responsible, to such extent as may be specified, for the enforcement of any of the relevant statutory provisions.*

(4) Health and safety regulations—
(a) may impose requirements by reference to the approval of [F36the Executive] or any other specified body or person;
(b) may provide for references in the regulations to any specified document to operate as reference to that document as revised or re-issued from time to time.

(5) Health and safety regulations—
(a) may provide (either unconditionally or subject to conditions, and with or without limit of time) for exemptions from any requirement or prohibition imposed by or under any of the relevant statutory provisions;
(b) may enable exemptions from any requirement or prohibition imposed by or under any of the relevant statutory provisions to be granted (either unconditionally or subject to conditions, and with or without limit of time) by any specified person or by any person authorised in that behalf by a specified authority.

(6) Health and safety regulations—
(a) may specify the persons or classes of persons who, in the event of a contravention of a requirement or prohibition imposed by or under the regulations, are to be guilty of an offence, whether in addition to or to the exclusion of other persons or classes of persons;
(b) may provide for any specified defence to be available in proceedings for any offence under the relevant statutory provisions either generally or in specified circumstances;
(c) may exclude proceedings on indictment in relation to offences consisting of a contravention of a requirement or prohibition imposed by or under any of the existing statutory provisions, sections 2 to 9 or health and safety regulations;
(d) may restrict the punishments [F37(other than the maximum fine on conviction on indictment)] which can be imposed in respect of any such offence as is mentioned in paragraph (c) above.

[F38(e)
F39. . . . .]
(7) Without prejudice to section 35, health and safety regulations may make provision for enabling offences under any of the relevant

statutory provisions to be treated as having been committed at any specified place for the purpose of bringing any such offence within the field of responsibility of any enforcing authority or conferring jurisdiction on any court to entertain proceedings for any such offence.

(8) Health and safety regulations may take the form of regulations applying to particular circumstances only or to a particular case only (for example, regulations applying to particular premises only).

47

Civil liability.

(1) Nothing in this Part shall be construed—
(a) as conferring a right of action in any civil proceedings in respect of any failure to comply with any duty imposed by sections 2 to 7 or any contravention of section 8; or
(b) as affecting the extent (if any) to which breach of a duty imposed by any of the existing statutory provisions is actionable; or
(c) as affecting the operation of section 12 of the ***M14****Nuclear Installations Act 1965 (right to compensation by virtue of certain provisions of that Act).*

(2) Breach of a duty imposed by health and safety regulations ***F132****. . . shall, so far as it causes damage, be actionable except in so far as the regulations provide otherwise.*

(3) No provision made by virtue of section 15(6)(b) shall afford a defence in any civil proceedings, whether brought by virtue of subsection (2) above or not; but as regards any duty imposed as mentioned in subsection (2) above health and safety regulations ***F132****. . . may provide for any defence specified in the regulations to be available in any action for breach of that duty.*

(4) Subsections (1)(a) and (2) above are without prejudice to any right of action which exists apart from the provisions of this Act, and subsection (3) above is without prejudice to any defence which may

be available apart from the provisions of the regulations there mentioned.

*(5) Any term of an agreement which purports to exclude or restrict the operation of subsection (2) above, or any liability arising by virtue of that subsection shall be void, except in so far as health and safety regulations **F132**. . . provide otherwise.*

(6) In this section "damage" includes the death of, or injury to, any person (including any disease and any impairment of a person's physical or mental condition).

Thus, as can be seen, it was since 1974, that statutory duties were imposed upon employers, which in turn imposed civil liabilities for breaches of the various employment Regulations, which will be dealt with separately in this book. This has arguably been a policy decision, of a Conservative Government, to reduce the burden of compensation claims upon employers.

How will the changes to Section 69 work in practice?

Section 69 of ERRA 2013 is going to have a number of important changes for those handling Employers' Liability claims. Some of these are as follows:-

1. It is important to remember that the duties imposed by the various Regulations will still apply. Indeed, the Courts, when determining whether there has been a breach of the common law duty of care will likely still look to the Regulations to what duties the Regulations are imposed upon an employer. However, a breach of a Regulation itself will not impose civil liability.

2. In order for a Claimant to prove a claim in common law negligence, the risk must have been reasonably foreseeable. The number of claims that would previously have succeeded under strict liability, pursuant to the Regulations, prior to Section 69 of ERRA 2013, especially claims under PUWER, may now be reduced, for risks

that were not foreseeable. This is discussed in more detail but it prudent to say here that at common law, the overall test for negligence is that of *'the reasonable and prudent employer taking positive thought for the safety of his workers in light of what he knows or ought to know.' (Stokes v Guest (1968) 1WLR 1886).* This will be discussed in more detail in later Chapters.

3. The changes undoubtedly mean that it will be more difficult for Claimants to succeed in Employers' Liability claims. The changes mean that it is more important than ever for the Claimant's Solicitor to consider whether a common law breach of a duty of care is likely to be established, and if it cannot be, close the claim, as it will fail at Trial.

4. It is important to remember that even where breaches of the Regulations impose strict liability, it will still be important to consider the Regulations and plead the Regulations in the Particulars of Claim, as guidance to the likely standard of duty to be applied by the Court at Trial. All too often all the Regulations are pleaded in either the Claim Notification Form or the Particulars of Claim, or not at all. It is important to consider, which specific Regulations are likely to apply and apply the same to the particular factors of a case. All the Regulations are considered in detail in other Chapters.

5. It is very important to remember that the Regulations only apply to accidents occurring on or after 1 October 2013. Although the old cases are now running out, it is important to note that in any case where the date of the accident is before 1 October 2013, some Regulations still impose strict liability and breach of some Regulations impose civil liability, so it is essential that these are still pleaded in the Particulars of Claim, where appropriate.

6. It may be argued that there will be an increased need for expert evidence in areas such as engineering as claimants try to meet the requirement of showing what happened and why it was negligent. The provision of engineering evidence in various types of accidents will be discussed in other Chapters and this will be an area this book will look at in detail.

CHAPTER SIX
CAUSATION INVESTIGATIONS

Causation is one of the most important aspects when considering any Employers' Liability claim and it is no different in a disease claim. The reason for this is of course that even if the claimant can succeed on the issue of breach of duty the claimant still has to prove causation in relation to the injuries sustained subject to the exception set out in ***Fairchild v Glenhaven Funeral Services Ltd*** [2002] UKHL 22 for asbestos cases as applied to lung cancer cases in *Carl Heneghan (Son & Executor of James Leo Heneghan, Deceased) v Manchester Dry Docks Ltd & Ors* [2016] EWCA Civ 86. This becomes even more important when the credibility of the claimant is at issue between the parties.

The claimant will have to prove legal and medical causation on the balance of probability. Establishing causation at an early stage in the case will be as important as establishing breach of duty, given that if the claimant's case fails on the issues of causation, there is little point in establishing breach of duty in the first instance.

This chapter will therefore concentrate solely on investigating causation in relation to employer's liability claims and focuses on the early investigations to be undertaken in relation to such cases at the outset.

Early Investigation

Early investigation of causation is always going to be key in relation to an Employers' Liability case. This will be particularly important if the defendant puts you on notice that causation is going to be an issue.

This inevitably leads to the question, as to how causation can be investigated in relation to such a case at an early stage, and, how can it be investigated economically, particularly with reference to fixed costs and portal costs that have been discussed in chapters one and two of this book.

The issue of causation can be investigated economically in the following ways:-

Medical Causation

(a) The claimant's solicitor will wish to obtain the claimant's general practitioner records and hospital records at the first opportunity. The claimant's solicitor should carefully go through the claimant's contemporaneous GP and hospital records as this will often provide clues as to the mechanism of the accident / exposure.

(b) The claimant's Solicitor will also likely wish to obtain a copy of the HSE reports and any witness evidence to check the mechanism of the accident exposure is consistent with how the claimant says it occurred.

(c) HMRCC and occupational health records are going to key in an Employers' Liability Disease case. injury imposed in negligence at common law then pleading the additional head of liability may confer no additional benefit but there may be circumstances in which 1 head of liability may confer no additional benefit but there may be circumstances in which

CHAPTER SEVEN

VIBRATION WHITE FINGER ('VWF') / HAND ARM VIBRATION SYNDROME ('HAVS') CASES – BREACH OF DUTY, CAUSATION AND QUANTUM

Dates of Knowledge

Defendants will only be liable for exposing workers to harmful conditions after they knew or ought to have known that such exposure was dangerous to health.

It is important to understand that this is a matter of law for the court to decide and not a question for the engineer. Many engineers give their opinion in this respect in their reports and naturally courts often accept and adopt such opinions. However, if the engineer's opinion is unhelpful to the claimant's case it can be challenged by reference to previous similar cases and by reference to the literature that was commonly available to the industry at the time when the claimant was exposed.

It is vital to any industrial disease claim that the engineering expert instructed for the claimant is utterly reliable and predictable in this respect, as an unhelpful date of knowledge can destroy a claim at a relatively late stage of proceedings, wasting sometimes years of work conducted up to that point. Feedback between colleagues on how an expert performs is part of ensuring positive reports.

The burden of proof is always on the claimant to prove that the defendant was in breach of duty by exposing him to excessive levels of noise or vibration. This usually requires engineering evidence. As exposure in such cases usually occurred up to 20 plus years before bringing the claim, it is usually not possible to take direct measurements of exposure *in situ* at the work place.

In vibration claims this is not usually a problem because, so long as the various tools which the claimant used can be identified, it is relatively easy for an engineer to calculate levels of exposure predicated upon hypothetical durations of exposure, obtained from the claimant and other witnesses.

Medical Evidence

Medical causation for VWF/HAVS is commonly the issue which is defended the most hotly. This is because there are a number of different constitutional causes of VWF/HAVS and because, outside of VWF/HAVS, age induced hearing loss is almost always a factor in deafness claims.

What are HAVS cases?

http://www.hse.gov.uk/vibration/hav/index.htm says:

> *Hand-arm vibration comes from the use of hand-held power tools and is the cause of significant ill health (painful and disabling disorders of the blood vessels, nerves and joints).*
>
> - *HAVS is preventable, but once the damage is done it is permanent.*
> - *HAVS is serious and disabling, and nearly 2 million people are at risk.*
> - *Damage from HAVS can include the inability to do fine work and can trigger painful finger blanching attacks.*
> - *The costs to employees and to employers of inaction could be high.*
> - *There are simple and cost-effective ways to eliminate risk of HAVS.*
> - *The Control of Vibration at Work Regulations focusses on the elimination or control of vibration exposure.*
> - *The long-term aim is to prevent new cases of HAVS occurring and enable workers to remain at work without disability.*

- *The most efficient and effective way of controlling exposure to hand-arm vibration is to look for new or alternative work methods which eliminate or reduce exposure to vibration.*
- *Health surveillance is vital to detect and respond to early signs of damage*

Hand arm vibration can be a significant health risk wherever powered hand tools are used for significant lengths of time. This is especially so in foundries construction and heavy fabrication including ship building. These are solutions to help you manage risks in your workplace.

Health and Safety Executive ('HSE') has identified some established good practice controls that can help to eliminate or reduce vibration risk in these industries and in others. HSE inspectors are promoting these controls during inspections in these sectors and will expect to see evidence of the elimination of vibration risks or of their reduction to the lowest level that is reasonably practicable. Where vibration risks remain, inspectors will be looking for evidence that the risks are being managed adequately and that suitable health surveillance is in place. Follow the industry links below for information on established good practice for managing HAV risks.

The Relevant Legislation in Force – Breach of Duty- HAVS / VWF

- Construction (Working Places) Places 1966.
- Management of Health and Safety at Work Regulations 1999.
- Workplace (Health, Safety and Welfare) Regulations 1992 (hereinafter referred to as the `Workplace Regulations')
- Manual Handling Operations Regulations 1992 (hereinafter referred to as the 'Handling Regulations'
- The Provision and use of Work Equipment Regulations 1992 (hereinafter referred to as the `Equipment Regulations')

Likely question on breach of duty

The following are useful questions to be asked of the Claimant in order to investigate breach of duty:

1. Was the claimant required to work for long periods with vibrating tools?
2. How often was the claimant required to use these tools and over what period?
3. Was the claimant provided with occupational screening?
4. Was the claimant provided with routine health surveillance?
5. Was the claimant warned of the risk of exposure to vibration?
6. Was the claimant warned about any risks associated with use of vibration tools?
7. Did the employer set the levels of vibration for which the claimant was subject to?
8. Was there a system of job rotation?
9. Was there a limit on the number of hours the tools could be used for?
10. Did the employer take expert evidence or advice on the use of vibrating tools/ equipment?
11. Did the employer examine the claimant's hands?
12. Did the employer warn the claimant about to the common signs of HAVs syndrome?
13. Was there a risk assessment in place under Regulation 3 of the Management Regulations?
14. Was the claimant provided with tools with lower vibration to enable work to be carried out?
15. Did the Defendant investigate other ways of minimising exposure?

In addition to above, there are also a number of papers that are relevant in terms of breach of duty:-

1. 1906- The Government enquiries were made upon the effects of use of pneumatic hammers and other tools used by workmen.

2. 1925 the Chief Inspector of Factories referred to the physical effects of pneumatic tools and use of VWF in users of vibrating tools/

3. Industrial Injuries Advisory Council in respect of vibration.

4. Report entitled VWF and Industry published in or about December 1973.

5. The BSI publication 'Guide to Evaluation and exposure to Human Hand – Arm System to Vibration (1975)

6. The Department of Environmental Services Street Scene Publication SWG 001 Rev1.

Nature of VWF/HAVS

Like deafness this is a cumulative condition but with a significant difference. That is that people are said to have a reservoir of tolerance to vibration, which once used up results in symptoms arising. There is no equivalent reservoir of tolerance in deafness cases. Thus, a person may be exposed to excessive vibration for a period of many years and have no symptoms at all. The person may then move to another employer where they have excessive exposure for a short period, but which uses up the remainder of their reservoir of tolerance causing symptoms to occur. We shall see later that this causes difficulties in apportionment as between different employers and as between exposure with one employer where some exposure was before the date of knowledge and some after.

In 1985 VWF became a prescribed condition, defined as '*episodic blanching of at least the two distal phalanges of the three or more fingers of one hand occurring throughout the year.*

There are three main standards in the industry which provide guidance to employers:

- **DD43, "A Guide to the Evaluation of Exposure of the Human Hand-Arm System to Vibration", British Standards Institution, 1975.**

This suggested maximum vibration levels beyond which exposure was thought to be unsafe. It recommended cumulative exposure time should never exceed 400 minutes per day, and for intermediate periods between 150 and 400 minutes there should be some interpolation. This also applied to workers using tools for less than 150 minutes per day.

- **BS 6842, "British Standard Guide to Measurement and Evaluation of Human Exposure to Vibration Transmitted to the Hand", 1987.**

This standard is the most important in VWF litigation. It sets out guidelines of prevention measures which are discussed below.

- **HS(G)88, Health and Safety Executive Guidance Booklet, 1994.**

HS(G)88 laid down an Action Level, derived from BS 6842. It states that any vibration exposure regularly exceeding 2.8m/s2 A(8) (meaning 2.8 metres per second, per second, with A(8) meaning the acceleration period averaged over an 8 hour period) should be assessed and preventative measures should be instituted. The measures include identifying potential hazards, calculating exposure time, implementing a risk reduction programme, instituting health surveillance and auditing and managing exposure i.e., policy, job rotation etc.

Once it has been shown that a defendant is in breach of duty by exposing a claimant to levels of vibration above the guideline maxima then there is a duty on the defendant to reduce that exposure and then the burden of proof is on defendant to show why it would be impractical to do so; *Brown & Ors v Corus (UK) Ltd* EWCA [2004] Civ 374 *per* Scott baker LJ. Para 34. Speculation as to what would have happened had D employed an engineer is inappropriate and in any event, it is submitted that the result of any adequate assessment would have been to implement the safety measures so clearly set out in the Vibration Guidelines.

An issue that often arises in relation to whether the claimant's exposure was in breach of duty is, whether there was 'regular' exposure above the guideline maxima. That is eminently a jury point for the judge, but it is my view that 'regular' is likely to mean frequently to the tune of two or three times per week for most weeks of the year.

Diagnosis Issues

There is no objective scientific test to diagnose HAVS. Diagnosis is made on the basis of:

a) The history of symptoms provided by the patient;
b) The history of relevant and significant vibration exposure, and;
c) No evidence of any underlying constitutional disorder to account for the symptoms other than vibration.

Defendants almost always seek to defend VWF/HAVS claims vigorously on medical causation, generally because there are many possible causes of Raynaud's phenomenon. These include medical conditions, exposure to the cold, heavy smoking and alcohol consumption, raised cholesterol and emotional events.

There are other difficulties with the diagnosis of VWF/HAVS:

- The claimant is unlikely to have an attack during medical examination in the warm consulting room and the doctor is dependent on the claimant's description of his symptoms.

- There is variability in the manifestations of the vibration-induced condition, the symptoms of which do not begin to manifest themselves for several years after exposure begins. This latent period varies according to severity of the exposure and the claimant's personal susceptibility.

- The vascular symptoms of the episodic whiteness and numbness, virtually identical to the symptoms caused by the occupational condition, occur naturally in 5% of men and 15% of women. There is no clear way to distinguish between the two.

- It is difficult to attribute the sensorineural and musculoskeletal symptoms to vibration as these can occur naturally as a result of the constitutional conditions.

- The insurance industry believes it is faced with many fraudulent claimants, who have learnt from co-workers how to give a convincing account of the symptoms and some judges are of this opinion as well. As for the latter point this is an important risk of the litigation and should not be under-estimated when considering any offers to settle.

Consequently, the defendant will seek to show in the medical evidence and through cross-examination that the symptoms described by the claimant are inconsistent with classic VWF/HAVS symptoms. The duration, pattern and distribution of attacks can be difficult for claimants to recall and this is one of the most fraught times for the claim.

In *Morgan v Corus* (2005) Unreported, Cardiff CC, No.4DFO5485 H.H.J. Graham Jones explored this issue of diagnosis and medical evidence. It was held that the relevant considerations in these cases were;

a) Whether there was exposure to vibrating equipment,
b) The claimant's descriptions of his symptoms,
c) The nature of the symptoms described and clinical findings and,
d) Other causes for the symptoms.

If there was significant exposure to vibration over a significant period and the claimant described symptoms which were sufficiently compatible with the range of symptoms and there were no other competing causes, then the claim would be established. It would not make a difference if the claimant did not exhibit all the classic syndromes and it would not matter if some symptoms were anomalous. Clearly this is a very helpful case for claimants and comes from the then Designated Civil Judge for Cardiff, however, it is not a binding authority being only County Court level.

Once again, the best advice is to employ an authoritative and reliable expert as cases are so often won and lost by the experts. If the Defendant is asserting that the condition is not VWF/HAVS but rather some unknown or unidentified connective tissue disorder (a common plea by defendants) then it may be wise to instruct a specialist rheumatologist. A consultant rheumatologist will carry more weight than a so-called expert on VWF in matter of pure rheumatology such as the issue of connective tissue disorders.

Foreseeability / Date of Knowledge

The dates of knowledge in VWF/HAVS cases vary between industries and because many of the cases draw a distinction between date of knowledge of risk and the institution of precautions to reduce or eliminate that risk. Whether the failure to take a particular precaution once knowledge is gained is a breach, will depend upon which step is under consideration. For example, there is no difficulty in issuing warnings and instructions to employees as soon as the risk is appreciated, but it would be unreasonable to expect the employer, particularly if a smaller firm, to immediately change his machinery.

Dates of knowledge and precautions have been found as follows in particular industries:

- *Fitter/Polisher* – Date of knowledge 1979
- *Rail Industry* – Date of knowledge 1973, Precaution of issuing warnings 1973, Precaution of periodical medical surveillance 1974
- *Coal Industry* – Date of knowledge 1973, Precaution of issuing warnings and undertaking medical surveillance 1975, Duty to

undertake job rotation 1976, Duty to adapt tools – Unspecified time thereafter

- *Gas Industry* – Date of knowledge 1975
- *Ship Repair Industry (Boilermaker)* – Date of knowledge 1975, Precautionary measures 1977
- *Woodworking Industry* – Date of knowledge 1991/1992
- *Farming Industry (Chainsaw Vibration)* – Date of knowledge 1992

In any case it will assist if a precedent can be found establishing a relevant date of knowledge. In the absence of this expert evidence as to the knowledge within a particular industry at a particular time may assist and as would historical development of knowledge of the VWF/HAVS condition.

Case Management

Preparation of a VWF/HAVS case should be done in three stages, each taken separately.

1. Taking full instructions from the claimant; working life and the tools used, information on the employers' date of knowledge, the client's symptoms, his general health and knowledge, witnesses and benefits he receives.

Working Life

- Obtain all information about earlier work, including accurate dates and information on the tools used. If the claimant cannot remember dates or employers, obtaining a HMR.C/DSS work history is recommended.

Employers' knowledge

- For each relevant employer it will be necessary to know whether any warnings were given, if there were any employment medicals and what they looked at, whether a HAVS questionnaire was completed, whether during employment the client was a union member and whether they provided information.

Symptoms and General Health

- The symptoms are usually tingling, numbness and blanching and not usually anything else. A description should be taken of the areas of tingling and numbness.

- It is important to remember that other things can cause symptoms of Raynaud's phenomenon; therefore, it is important to take a note of any medical conditions and prescribed drugs.

- A date must be taken of when the client first noted his symptoms. If he became aware of symptoms soon after first exposure, then he may have an underlying constitutional disorder.

- A history of post-liability worsening should be obtained, where a client has exposure pre and post-liability date, and where he has onset symptoms before that date.

Witnesses

- The client should be asked for the names of any witnesses in relation to his use of tools at work (managers and colleagues), and the difficulties he has in his everyday life (spouse/partners and helpers).

2. Obtaining medical evidence

Once there is clear proof from the client the next stage is to obtain a medical report from a vascular surgeon. GP notes and records must be obtained to send to the consultant.

In making a diagnosis all a consultant can do is exclude any constitutional medical factor that may have caused the symptoms and take a comprehensive work history before diagnosing. It is important to be clear to the consultant on anything of concern. If apportionment is likely to be relevant, ask the consultant to deal with this.

The consultant is not a vibration expert and if the engineering evidence is to the effect that the tools did not vibrate or vibrate sufficiently, clearly the claim cannot continue. It is therefore important to consider whether it is better to ask for engineering evidence prior to a diagnosis.

The consultant should be able to assess the claimant's degree of disability on both the Taylor-Pelmear and Stockholm Scales. This is relevant to quantum. If the consultant cannot do this he should not be used.

Once the medical report is received the following should be checked:

a) the accuracy of the description of tools and employment
b) any relevant medical history obtained
c) whether the diagnosis is wholly VWF/HAVS and if not what proportion is,
d) the grading on both scales
e) handicap on the labour market
f) if apportionment is an issue the disability on the relevant date
g) whether Carpal Tunnel Syndrome is mentioned.

Classification of VWF/HAVS

For many years the standard classification was the Taylor-Pelmear Scale, developed in the 1960s and 1970s. This scale contained difficulties and, as detailed below, it is now regarded as obsolete.

The Taylor Pelmear Scale

Stage 0 No symptoms.

Stage 0_T Intermittent tingling, but no interference with work, domestic or social activities.

Stage 0_N Intermittent numbness, but no interference with work, domestic or social activities.

Stage $0_T/0_N$	Intermittent tingling and numbness, but no interference with work, domestic or social activities.
Stage 1	Blanching during winter of one or more finger-tips without any interference with work, domestic or social activities.
Stage 2	Blanching during winter characterised by increased frequency and number of fingers affected, usually triggered by cold. The blanching area extends beyond the finger-tips to the mid-phalangeal joints and often to the base of the fingers. There is slight interference with domestic and social activities but not with work.
Stage 3	Extensive blanching with frequent episodes in summer as well as in winter. There is definite interference with work, domestic and social activities.
Stage 4	Extensive blanching affecting all digits in summer as well as in winter, leading to a change of occupation.

In 1986 the Stockholm Workshop Scale was defined to assess the vascular and neurological components. It is commonly considered now that the Taylor-Pelmear Scale is obsolete but the courts do still sometimes take it into account.

The Stockholm Scales

1. Vascular Component

STAGE	GRADE	DESCRIPTION
0		No attacks.
1	Mild	Occasional attacks affecting only the tips of one or more fingers.
2	Moderate	Occasional attacks affecting distal and middle

		(rarely also proximal) phalanges of one or more fingers.
3	Severe	Frequent attacks affecting all phalanges of most fingers.
4	Very severe	As in stage 3, with tropic changes in the finger tips.

2. Neurological Component

STAGE	DESCRIPTION
0SN	Vibration-exposed but no symptoms.
1SN	Intermittent numbness with or without tingling.
2SN	Intermittent or persistent numbness, reduced sensory perception.
3SN	Intermittent or persistent numbness, reduced tactile discrimination and/or manipulative dexterity.

Example: 3R(4)/2L(1) means that, on the vascular scale, the right hand is at stage 3 with 4 digits affected, while the left hand is at stage 2 with 1 digit affected.

Prognosis and Reversibility of Symptoms

Early research showed that symptoms of VWF/HAVS would persist despite cessation of the vibration exposure and the disease had more tendency to progress than regress once it had developed. However, this has since been questioned.

Vascular Symptoms

Studies have confirmed that the prevalence of vascular symptoms of VWF diminish when vibration exposure ceases or is reduced in forestry workers.

A large study has shown that the percentage prevalence of vascular symptoms fell to 50 percent 12 years after vibration exposure ceased. The reduction was dependent on the initial stage of the disorder, the period of exposure after the onset of symptoms and age at the time exposure ceased.

Neurological Symptoms

There is some evidence to say that there may be some improvement when vibration exposure ceases and any improvement is dependent on the level of vibration exposure and age of the individual concerned.

Apportionment of Damages

As described above there is often an issue with the apportionment of damages either as between defendants or as between periods of negligent and non-negligent exposure. This is because a straight-line apportionment approach can do injustice to the claimant due to the nature of the reservoir of tolerance being used up.

There are conflicting authorities on whether straight-line apportionment should be used or not. I set out here a basic argument that favours a claimant who wishes the court to ignore non-negligent exposure that used up his reservoir of tolerance.

It is submitted that there should be no reduction in damages for the period of exposure prior to the claimant being symptomatic. The non-negligent exposure to vibration evidently used up the claimant's reservoir of tolerance to vibration but, as symptoms did not start until after the date of knowledge it is submitted that the actual harm to the claimant that is being compensated for has been caused by the negligent exposure. But for that continued exposure the claimant would not have had symptoms. In support of the submission that no deduction from the claimant's damages should be made for prior non-negligent exposure the claimant relies on the following cases:

i. *Smith v Wright & Beyer* in which Pill LJ at paragraph 14, with whom Tuckey J agreed, rejected the submission that a discount should be applied to damages to take into account previous non-negligent exposure that used up the Reservoir of the claimant.

ii. In *Brookes v (1) South Yorkshire Passenger Transport Executive (2) Mainline Group* [2005] EWCA Civ. 452 the court agreed with this approach stating, at paragraph 26, that where symptoms first arose after the date of knowledge despite some previous exposure then the claimant may properly argue that he should receive full damages on the basis that he would never have developed any symptoms had it not been for the defendant's negligence. If it is the defendant's contention that symptoms do not get worse after exposure to vibration has ceased it follows that, if the defendant is correct, then the claimant would not have developed the condition if his exposure had been stopped before he became symptomatic.

iii. Despite the fact that the Court of Appeal upheld the decision by Smith J in *Allen v British Rail Engineering Ltd* [2001] PIQR Q101 that damages could be reduced by taking into account exposure to vibration that had been non-negligent this was in relation to when symptoms had started to show. Their Lordships in *Brookes* stated, at paragraph 26 that if there is insufficient evidence before the court to calculate the appropriate amount of such a reduction then damages should be awarded in full to the claimant on the basis that the defendant's negligence had made a material contribution to the condition.

iv. Where there is such evidence Neuberger LJ in *Rugby Joinery v Whitfield* [2005] EWCA Civ 561 held at paragraph 52 that an apportionment based by reference to time could not have been criticised but that a straight-line apportionment would have been grossly unfair to the claimant. At paragraph 52 His Lordship states that it would be quite unrealistic to give the same weight to the earlier years and in particular as to the years after symptoms arose.

v. It is submitted that even where the court is satisfied that some symptoms would have started even if exposure had ceased prior to the date of knowledge, the approach of the Court of Appeal is that damages will be assessed by assessing the total damages that the condition at trial merits and taking away from this the amount that would have been ascribed to the severity of the condition as at the date of knowledge. It is submitted that where there is simply insufficient medical evidence on this point for the court to make any sensible and principled reduction on this basis no reduction should be made.

vi. Further and additionally it is submitted that there is an additional argument that the defendant in such a case must be liable for the entirety of damages with no discount for the previous exposure using up the claimant's reservoir based on legal principle. This is the principle that a tortfeasor must take his victim as he finds him. Where a claimant has had his reservoir used up albeit non-negligently he is then particularly vulnerable to further exposure. It follows that the eggshell skull rule applies in such cases and that the claimant should recover damages in full. The guidance in HS(G) 88 at paragraph 87 clearly states that employers must conduct pre-employment assessment of workers and it is submitted that this shows that a higher duty is owed to those who may have been exposed to vibration before any duty on a particular employer arose.

Quantum

(J) Vibration White Finger (VWF) and/or Hand Arm Vibration Syndrome (HAVS)

[10.9]

Vibration White Finger and/or Hand Arm Vibration Syn-drome, caused by exposure to vibration, is a slowly progres-sive condition, the development and severity of which are affected by the degree of exposure, in particular the magnitude, frequency, duration and transmission of the vibration. The symptoms are similar to those experienced in the constitution-al condition of Raynaud's phenomenon.

The Stockholm Workshop Scale is now the accepted table for medical grading of the severity of the condition. The Scale classifies both the vascular and sensorineural components in two complementary tables. Individual assessment is made separately for each hand and for each finger.

The vascular component is graded between Stage 0V (no at-tacks) through mild, moderate and severe to 4V (very severe) where there are frequent attacks affecting all phalanges of most fingers with atrophic changes in the fingertips. The sensori-neural component is graded between Stage 0SN (no symp-toms) and 3SN (intermittent or persistent numbness, reduced tactile discrimination and/or manipulative dexterity). The grade of disorder is indicated by the stage and number of af-fected fingers on both hands.

Any interference with work or social life is disregarded in that grading.

The assessment of damages is therefore not strictly tied to the Stockholm Workshop Scale grading. It depends more on the extent of the symptoms and their impact, having regard to the following factors:

(i) age at onset;

(ii) whether one or both hands are affected and, if only one, whether it is the dominant hand;

(iii) number of fingers affected;

(iv) extent of impaired dexterity and/or reduction in grip strength;

(v) frequency and duration of painful episodes;

(vi) effect of symptoms on work, domestic and social life.

Accordingly, depending on individual circumstances, a lower award might be made despite significant Stockholm Work-shop Scale grading where, eg, employment is unaffected, while a higher award might be attracted where there is a lesser grading but a greater impact on normal life.

In a severe case, the injury may be regarded as damaging a hand rather than being confined to the fingers.

The brackets can best be defined and valued as follows (note that it is not intended that these should correlate directly with the Stockholm Workshop Scale):

with 10% uplift

(a) Most Serious £24,050 to £29,200 £26,460 to £32,120

Persisting bilateral symptoms in a younger person which in-terfere significantly with daily life and lead to a change in employment. with 10% uplift

(b) Serious £12,750 to £24,050 £14,030 to £26,460

In this bracket there will have been a marked interference with work and domestic activity. Attacks may occur throughout the year.

(c) Moderate £6,575 to £12,750 £7,230 to £14,030

This bracket will include claimants in their middle years where employment has been maintained or varied only to re-move excess vibration. Attacks will occur mostly in cold weather.

(d) Minor £2,275 to £6,575 £2,500 to £7,230

Occasional symptoms in only a few fingers with a modest effect on work or leisure.

CHAPTER EIGHT
CONTROL OF SUBSTANCES HAZARDOUS TO HEALTH ('COSHH') AND RESPIRATORY CASES INCLUDING DUST / FUME EXPOSURE – BREACH OF DUTY, CAUSATION AND QUANTUM

Respiratory claims are one of the more obscure disease claims seen in practice. They are governed by COSHH - The Control of Substances Hazardous to Health Regulations. The 1998 Regulations applied from 1 October 1989. The 1994 Regulations applied from 16 January 1999. The 1999 Regulations came into force on 25 March 1999 and were replaced by the 2002 Regulations on 21 November 2002.

The 2002 Regulations set out:-

> ***Duties under these Regulations***
>
> *3.—(1) Where a duty is placed by these Regulations on an employer in respect of his employees, he shall, so far as is reasonably practicable, be under a like duty in respect of any other person, whether at work or not, who may be affected by the work carried out by the employer except that the duties of the employer—*
> *(a) under regulation 11 (health surveillance) shall not extend to persons who are not his employees; and*
> *(b) under regulations 10, 12(1) and (2) and 13 (which relate respectively to monitoring, information and training and dealing with accidents) shall not extend to persons who are not his employees, unless those persons are on the premises where the work is being carried out.*
>
> *(2) These Regulations shall apply to a self-employed person as they apply to an employer and an employee and as if that self-employed person were both an employer and an employee, except that regulations 10 and 11 shall not apply to a self-employed person.*

(3) The duties imposed by these Regulations shall not extend to the master or crew of a sea-going ship or to the employer of such persons in relation to the normal shipboard activities of a ship's crew under the direction of the master.

Prohibitions relating to certain substances

4.—(1) Those substances described in Column 1 of Schedule 2 are prohibited to the extent set out in the corresponding entry in Column 2 of that Schedule.

(2) The importation into the United Kingdom, other than from another member State, of the following substances and articles is prohibited, namely—
(a) 2-naphthylamine, benzidine, 4-aminodiphenyl, 4-nitrodiphenyl, their salts and any substance containing any of those compounds in a total concentration equal to or greater than 0.1 per cent by mass;
(b) matches made with white phosphorus,
and a contravention of this paragraph shall be punishable under the Customs and Excise Management Act 1979(1) and not as a contravention of a health and safety regulation.

(3) A person shall not supply during the course of or for use at work a substance or article specified in paragraph (2).

(4) A person shall not supply during the course of or for use at work, benzene or a substance containing benzene unless its intended use is not prohibited by item 11 of Schedule 2.

Application of regulations 6 to 13

5.—(1) ***Regulations 6 to 13 shall have effect with a view to protecting persons against a risk to their health, whether immediate or delayed, arising from exposure to substances hazardous to health except—***
(a) where and to the extent that the following Regulations apply, namely—
(i) the Coal Mines (Respirable Dust) Regulations 1975(1),

(ii) the Control of Lead at Work Regulations 2002(2),
(iii) the Control of Asbestos at Work Regulations 2002(3);
(b) where the substance is hazardous to health solely by virtue of its radioactive, explosive or flammable properties, or solely because it is at a high or low temperature or a high pressure;
(c) where the risk to health is a risk to the health of a person to whom the substance is administered in the course of his medical treatment.

(2) In paragraph (1)(c) "medical treatment" means medical or dental examination or treatment which is conducted by, or under the direction of a—
(a) registered medical practitioner;
(b) registered dentist; or
(c) other person who is an appropriate practitioner for the purposes of section 58 of the Medicines Act 1968(4),
and includes any such examination or treatment conducted for the purpose of research.
Assessment of the risk to health created by work involving substances hazardous to health

6.—(1) An employer shall not carry out work which is liable to expose any employees to any substance hazardous to health unless he has—
(a) made a suitable and sufficient assessment of the risk created by that work to the health of those employees and of the steps that need to be taken to meet the requirements of these Regulations; and
(b) implemented the steps referred to in sub-paragraph (a).

(2) The risk assessment shall include consideration of—
(a) the hazardous properties of the substance;
(b) information on health effects provided by the supplier, including information contained in any relevant safety data sheet;
(c) the level, type and duration of exposure;
(d) the circumstances of the work, including the amount of the substance involved;
(e) activities, such as maintenance, where there is the potential for a high level of exposure;

(f) any relevant occupational exposure standard, maximum exposure limit or similar occupational exposure limit;
(g) the effect of preventive and control measures which have been or will be taken in accordance with regulation 7;
(h) the results of relevant health surveillance;
(i) the results of monitoring of exposure in accordance with regulation 10;
(j) in circumstances where the work will involve exposure to more than one substance hazardous to health, the risk presented by exposure to such substances in combination;
(k) the approved classification of any biological agent; and
(l) such additional information as the employer may need in order to complete the risk assessment.

(3) The risk assessment shall be reviewed regularly and forthwith if —

(a) there is reason to suspect that the risk assessment is no longer valid;
(b) there has been a significant change in the work to which the risk assessment relates; or
(c) the results of any monitoring carried out in accordance with regulation 10 show it to be necessary,
and where, as a result of the review, changes to the risk assessment are required, those changes shall be made.

(4) Where the employer employs 5 or more employees, he shall record
(a) the significant findings of the risk assessment as soon as is practicable after the risk assessment is made; and
(b) the steps which he has taken to meet the requirements of regulation 7.

Prevention or control of exposure to substances hazardous to health

7.—(1) Every employer shall ensure that the exposure of his employees to substances hazardous to health is either prevented or, where this is not reasonably practicable, adequately controlled.

(2) In complying with his duty of prevention under paragraph (1), substitution shall by preference be undertaken, whereby the employer shall avoid, so far as is reasonably practicable, the use of a substance hazardous to health at the workplace by replacing it with a substance or process which, under the conditions of its use, either eliminates or reduces the risk to the health of his employees.

(3) Where it is not reasonably practicable to prevent exposure to a substance hazardous to health, the employer shall comply with his duty of control under paragraph (1) by applying protection measures appropriate to the activity and consistent with the risk assessment, including, in order of priority—
(a) the design and use of appropriate work processes, systems and engineering controls and the provision and use of suitable work equipment and materials;
(b) the control of exposure at source, including adequate ventilation systems and appropriate organisational measures; and
(c) where adequate control of exposure cannot be achieved by other means, the provision of suitable personal protective equipment in addition to the measures required by sub-paragraphs (a) and (b).

(4) The measures referred to in paragraph (3) shall include—
(a) arrangements for the safe handling, storage and transport of substances hazardous to health, and of waste containing such substances, at the workplace;
(b) the adoption of suitable maintenance procedures;
(c) reducing, to the minimum required for the work concerned—
(i) the number of employees subject to exposure,
(ii) the level and duration of exposure, and
(iii) the quantity of substances hazardous to health present at the workplace;
(d) the control of the working environment, including appropriate general ventilation; and
(e) appropriate hygiene measures including adequate washing facilities.

(5) Without prejudice to the generality of paragraph (1), where it is not reasonably practicable to prevent exposure to a carcinogen, the

employer shall apply the following measures in addition to those required by paragraph (3)—
(a) totally enclosing the process and handling systems, unless this is not reasonably practicable;
(b) the prohibition of eating, drinking and smoking in areas that may be contaminated by carcinogens;
(c) cleaning floors, walls and other surfaces at regular intervals and whenever necessary;
(d) designating those areas and installations which may be contaminated by carcinogens and using suitable and sufficient warning signs; and
(e) storing, handling and disposing of carcinogens safely, including using closed and clearly labelled containers.

(6) Without prejudice to the generality of paragraph (1), where it is not reasonably practicable to prevent exposure to a biological agent, the employer shall apply the following measures in addition to those required by paragraph (3)—
(a) displaying suitable and sufficient warning signs, including the biohazard sign shown in Part IV of Schedule 3;
(b) specifying appropriate decontamination and disinfection procedures;
(c) instituting means for the safe collection, storage and disposal of contaminated waste, including the use of secure and identifiable containers, after suitable treatment where appropriate;
(d) testing, where it is necessary and technically possible, for the presence, outside the primary physical confinement, of biological agents used at work;
(e) specifying procedures for working with, and transporting at the workplace, a biological agent or material that may contain such an agent;
(f) where appropriate, making available effective vaccines for those employees who are not already immune to the biological agent to which they are exposed or are liable to be exposed;
(g) instituting hygiene measures compatible with the aim of preventing or reducing the accidental transfer or release of a biological agent from the workplace, including—

(i) the provision of appropriate and adequate washing and toilet facilities, and
(ii) where appropriate, the prohibition of eating, drinking, smoking and the application of cosmetics in working areas where there is a risk of contamination by biological agents; and
(h) where there are human patients or animals which are, or are suspected of being, infected with a Group 3 or 4 biological agent, the employer shall select the most suitable control and containment measures from those listed in Part II of Schedule 3 with a view to controlling adequately the risk of infection.

(7) Without prejudice to the generality of paragraph (1), where there is exposure to a substance for which a maximum exposure limit has been approved, control of exposure shall, so far as the inhalation of that substance is concerned, only be treated as being adequate if the level of exposure is reduced so far as is reasonably practicable and in any case below the maximum exposure limit.

(8) Without prejudice to the generality of paragraph (1), where there is exposure to a substance for which an occupational exposure standard has been approved, control of exposure shall, so far as the inhalation of that substance is concerned, only be treated as being adequate if—
(a) that occupational exposure standard is not exceeded; or
(b) where that occupational exposure standard is exceeded, the employer identifies the reasons for the standard being exceeded and takes appropriate action to remedy the situation as soon as is reasonably practicable.

(9) Personal protective equipment provided by an employer in accordance with this regulation shall be suitable for the purpose and shall —

(a) comply with any provision in the Personal Protective Equipment Regulations 2002(1) which is applicable to that item of personal protective equipment; or
(b) in the case of respiratory protective equipment, where no provision referred to in sub-paragraph (a) applies, be of a type approved

or shall conform to a standard approved, in either case, by the Executive.

(10) Without prejudice to the provisions of this regulation, Schedule 3 shall have effect in relation to work with biological agents.

(11) In this regulation, "adequate" means adequate having regard only to the nature of the substance and the nature and degree of exposure to substances hazardous to health and "adequately" shall be construed accordingly.

Use of control measures etc.

***8.**—(1) Every employer who provides any control measure, other thing or facility in accordance with these Regulations shall take all reasonable steps to ensure that it is properly used or applied as the case may be.*

(2) Every employee shall make full and proper use of any control measure, other thing or facility provided in accordance with these Regulations and, where relevant, shall—
(a) take all reasonable steps to ensure it is returned after use to any accommodation provided for it; and
(b) if he discovers a defect therein, report it forthwith to his employer.

Maintenance, examination and testing of control measures

***9.**—(1) Every employer who provides any control measure to meet the requirements of regulation 7 shall ensure that, where relevant, it is maintained in an efficient state, in efficient working order, in good repair and in a clean condition.*

(2) Where engineering controls are provided to meet the requirements of regulation 7, the employer shall ensure that thorough examination and testing of those controls is carried out—
(a) in the case of local exhaust ventilation plant, at least once every 14 months, or for local exhaust ventilation plant used in conjunction with a process specified in Column 1 of Schedule 4, at not more than

the interval specified in the corresponding entry in Column 2 of that Schedule; or
(b) in any other case, at suitable intervals.

(3) Where respiratory protective equipment (other than disposable respiratory protective equipment) is provided to meet the requirements of regulation 7, the employer shall ensure that thorough examination and, where appropriate, testing of that equipment is carried out at suitable intervals.

(4) Every employer shall keep a suitable record of the examinations and tests carried out in accordance with paragraphs (2) and (3) and of repairs carried out as a result of those examinations and tests, and that record or a suitable summary thereof shall be kept available for at least 5 years from the date on which it was made.

(5) Every employer shall ensure that personal protective equipment, including protective clothing, is:
(a) properly stored in a well-defined place;
(b) checked at suitable intervals; and
(c) when discovered to be defective, repaired or replaced before further use.

(6) Personal protective equipment which may be contaminated by a substance hazardous to health shall be removed on leaving the working area and kept apart from uncontaminated clothing and equipment.

(7) The employer shall ensure that the equipment referred to in paragraph (6) is subsequently decontaminated and cleaned or, if necessary, destroyed.

Monitoring exposure at the workplace

***10.**—(1) Where the risk assessment indicates that—*
(a) it is requisite for ensuring the maintenance of adequate control of the exposure of employees to substances hazardous to health; or
(b) it is otherwise requisite for protecting the health of employees,

the employer shall ensure that the exposure of employees to substances hazardous to health is monitored in accordance with a suitable procedure.

(2) Paragraph (1) shall not apply where the employer is able to demonstrate by another method of evaluation that the requirements of regulation 7(1) have been complied with.

(3) The monitoring referred to in paragraph (1) shall take place—
(a) at regular intervals; and
(b) when any change occurs which may affect that exposure.

(4) Where a substance or process is specified in Column 1 of Schedule 5, monitoring shall be carried out at least at the frequency specified in the corresponding entry in Column 2 of that Schedule.

(5) The employer shall ensure that a suitable record of monitoring carried out for the purpose of this regulation is made and maintained and that that record or a suitable summary thereof is kept available —

(a) where the record is representative of the personal exposures of identifiable employees, for at least 40 years; or
(b) in any other case, for at least 5 years,
from the date of the last entry made in it.

(6) Where an employee is required by regulation 11 to be under health surveillance, an individual record of any monitoring carried out in accordance with this regulation shall be made, maintained and kept in respect of that employee.

(7) The employer shall—
(a) on reasonable notice being given, allow an employee access to his personal monitoring record;
(b) provide the Executive with copies of such monitoring records as the Executive may require; and
(c) if he ceases to trade, notify the Executive forthwith in writing and make available to the Executive all monitoring records kept by him.
Health surveillance

11.—(1) Where it is appropriate for the protection of the health of his employees who are, or are liable to be, exposed to a substance hazardous to health, the employer shall ensure that such employees are under suitable health surveillance.

(2) Health surveillance shall be treated as being appropriate where—
(a) the employee is exposed to one of the substances specified in Column 1 of Schedule 6 and is engaged in a process specified in Column 2 of that Schedule, and there is a reasonable likelihood that an identifiable disease or adverse health effect will result from that exposure; or
(b) the exposure of the employee to a substance hazardous to health is such that—
(i) an identifiable disease or adverse health effect may be related to the exposure,
(ii) there is a reasonable likelihood that the disease or effect may occur under the particular conditions of his work, and
(iii) there are valid techniques for detecting indications of the disease or effect, and the technique of investigation is of low risk to the employee.

(3) The employer shall ensure that a health record, containing particulars approved by the Executive, in respect of each of his employees to whom paragraph (1) applies, is made and maintained and that that record or a copy thereof is kept available in a suitable form for at least 40 years from the date of the last entry made in it.

(4) The employer shall—
(a) on reasonable notice being given, allow an employee access to his personal health record;
(b) provide the Executive with copies of such health records as the Executive may require; and
(c) if he ceases to trade, notify the Executive forthwith in writing and make available to the Executive all health records kept by him.

(5) If an employee is exposed to a substance specified in Schedule 6 and is engaged in a process specified therein, the health surveillance required under paragraph (1) shall include medical surveillance

under the supervision of a relevant doctor at intervals of not more than 12 months or at such shorter intervals as the relevant doctor may require.

(6) Where an employee is subject to medical surveillance in accordance with paragraph (5) and a relevant doctor has certified by an entry in the health record of that employee that in his professional opinion that employee should not be engaged in work which exposes him to that substance or that he should only be so engaged under conditions specified in the record, the employer shall not permit the employee to be engaged in such work except in accordance with the conditions, if any, specified in the health record, unless that entry has been cancelled by a relevant doctor.

(7) Where an employee is subject to medical surveillance in accordance with paragraph (5) and a relevant doctor has certified by an entry in his health record that medical surveillance should be continued after his exposure to that substance has ceased, the employer shall ensure that the medical surveillance of that employee is continued in accordance with that entry while he is employed by the employer, unless that entry has been cancelled by a relevant doctor.

(8) An employee to whom this regulation applies shall, when required by his employer and at the cost of the employer, present himself during his working hours for such health surveillance procedures as may be required for the purposes of paragraph (1) and, in the case of an employee who is subject to medical surveillance in accordance with paragraph (5), shall furnish the relevant doctor with such information concerning his health as the relevant doctor may reasonably require.

(9) Where, as a result of health surveillance, an employee is found to have an identifiable disease or adverse health effect which is considered by a relevant doctor or other occupational health professional to be the result of exposure to a substance hazardous to health the employer of that employee shall—

(a) ensure that a suitably qualified person informs the employee accordingly and provides the employee with information and advice regarding further health surveillance;
(b) review the risk assessment;
(c) review any measure taken to comply with regulation 7, taking into account any advice given by a relevant doctor, occupational health professional or by the Executive;
(d) consider assigning the employee to alternative work where there is no risk of further exposure to that substance, taking into account any advice given by a relevant doctor or occupational health professional; and
(e) provide for a review of the health of any other employee who has been similarly exposed, including a medical examination where such an examination is recommended by a relevant doctor, occupational health professional or by the Executive.

(10) Where, for the purpose of carrying out his functions under these Regulations, a relevant doctor requires to inspect any workplace or any record kept for the purposes of these Regulations, the employer shall permit him to do so.

(11) Where an employee or an employer is aggrieved by a decision recorded in the health record by a relevant doctor to suspend an employee from work which exposes him to a substance hazardous to health (or to impose conditions on such work), he may, by an application in writing to the Executive within 28 days of the date on which he was notified of the decision, apply for that decision to be reviewed in accordance with a procedure approved for the purposes of this paragraph by the Health and Safety Commission, and the result of that review shall be notified to the employee and employer and entered in the health record in accordance with the approved procedure.

Information, instruction and training for persons who may be exposed to substances hazardous to health

12.—(1) Every employer who undertakes work which is liable to expose an employee to a substance hazardous to health shall provide that employee with suitable and sufficient information, instruction and training.

(2) Without prejudice to the generality of paragraph (1), the information, instruction and training provided under that paragraph shall include—
(a) details of the substances hazardous to health to which the employee is liable to be exposed including—
(i) the names of those substances and the risk which they present to health,
(ii) any relevant occupational exposure standard, maximum exposure limit or similar occupational exposure limit,
(iii) access to any relevant safety data sheet, and
(iv) other legislative provisions which concern the hazardous properties of those substances;
(b) the significant findings of the risk assessment;
(c) the appropriate precautions and actions to be taken by the employee in order to safeguard himself and other employees at the workplace;
(d) the results of any monitoring of exposure in accordance with regulation 10 and, in particular, in the case of a substance hazardous to health for which a maximum exposure limit has been approved, the employee or his representatives shall be informed forthwith, if the results of such monitoring show that the maximum exposure limit has been exceeded;
(e) the collective results of any health surveillance undertaken in accordance with regulation 11 in a form calculated to prevent those results from being identified as relating to a particular person; and
(f) where employees are working with a Group 4 biological agent or material that may contain such an agent, the provision of written instructions and, if appropriate, the display of notices which outline the procedures for handling such an agent or material.

(3) The information, instruction and training required by paragraph (1) shall be—
(a) adapted to take account of significant changes in the type of work carried out or methods of work used by the employer; and

(b) provided in a manner appropriate to the level, type and duration of exposure identified by the risk assessment.

(4) Every employer shall ensure that any person (whether or not his employee) who carries out work in connection with the employer's duties under these Regulations has suitable and sufficient information, instruction and training.

(5) Where containers and pipes for substances hazardous to health used at work are not marked in accordance with any relevant legislation listed in Schedule 7, the employer shall, without prejudice to any derogations provided for in that legislation, ensure that the contents of those containers and pipes, together with the nature of those contents and any associated hazards, are clearly identifiable.

Arrangements to deal with accidents, incidents and emergencies

13.—(1) Subject to paragraph (4) and without prejudice to the relevant provisions of the Management of Health and Safety at Work Regulations 1999(1), in order to protect the health of his employees from an accident, incident or emergency related to the presence of a substance hazardous to health at the workplace, the employer shall ensure that—
(a) procedures, including the provision of appropriate first-aid facilities and relevant safety drills (which shall be tested at regular intervals), have been prepared which can be put into effect when such an event occurs;
(b) information on emergency arrangements, including—
(i) details of relevant work hazards and hazard identification arrangements, and
(ii) specific hazards likely to arise at the time of an accident, incident or emergency, is available; and
(c) suitable warning and other communication systems are established to enable an appropriate response, including remedial actions and rescue operations, to be made immediately when such an event occurs.

(2) The employer shall ensure that information on the procedures and systems required by paragraph (1)(a) and (c) and the information required by paragraph(1)(b) is—
(a) made available to relevant accident and emergency services to enable those services, whether internal or external to the workplace, to prepare their own response procedures and precautionary measures; and
(b) displayed at the workplace, if this is appropriate.

(3) Subject to paragraph (4), in the event of an accident, incident or emergency related to the presence of a substance hazardous to health at the workplace, the employer shall ensure that—
(a) immediate steps are taken to—
(i) mitigate the effects of the event,
(ii) restore the situation to normal, and
(iii) inform those of his employees who may be affected;
(b) only those persons who are essential for the carrying out of repairs and other necessary work are permitted in the affected area and they are provided with—
(i) appropriate personal protective equipment, and
(ii) any necessary specialised safety equipment and plant,which shall be used until the situation is restored to normal; and
(c) in the case of an incident or accident which has or may have resulted in the release of a biological agent which could cause severe human disease, as soon as practicable thereafter his employees or their representatives are informed of—
(i) the causes of that incident or accident, and
(ii) the measures taken or to be taken to rectify the situation.

(4) Paragraph (1) and, provided the substance hazardous to health is not a carcinogen or biological agent, paragraph (3) shall not apply where—
(a) the results of the risk assessment show that, because of the quantity of each substance hazardous to health present at the workplace, there is only a slight risk to the health of employees; and
(b) the measures taken by the employer to comply with the duty under regulation 7(1) are sufficient to control that risk.

(5) An employee shall report forthwith, to his employer or to any other employee of that employer with specific responsibility for the health and safety of his fellow employees, any accident or incident which has or may have resulted in the release of a biological agent which could cause severe human disease.

Other Statutory Provisions

- Personal Protective Equipment at Work Regulations 1992 (the PPE Regulations).
- The Management of Health & Safety at Work Regulations 1992 ('the 1992 Health Regulations'),
- Health and Safety at Work Act 1974 ('Health and Safety Regulations'),
- The Workplace (Health, Safety & Welfare) Regulations 1992 ('the Workplace Regulations'),
- The Management of Health & Safety Regulations 1999, ('the Safety Regulations').

A Worked Example – Breach of Duty

Asthma Exposure in the Workplace Caused by UPVC dust

The following may be relevant:-

The Health & Safety at Work Act 1974

(i) Failed to comply with Section 2(1) to ensure the health, safety and welfare of the Claimant;
(ii) Failed to comply with Section 2(2) to maintain a safe system of work without risks to health;

The Management of Health & Safety at Work Regulations 1992

(i) Failed to discharge its duty under Regulation 3 in that they did not make a suitable and sufficient assessment of the health and safety risks to which the Claimant was exposed and failed to review any such assessment;
(ii) Failed to discharge its duty under Regulation 4 in that they did not give effect to appropriate arrangements for the effective planning, organisation, control, monitoring and review of preventative and protective measures;
(iii) Failed to discharge its duty under Regulation 6 in that they did not appoint a competent person to assist the Defendant to undertake the necessary measures to comply with its obligations under the Regulations;
(iv) Failed to discharge its duty under Regulation 8 in that they did not provide the Claimant with comprehensible and relevant information on:
(a) the risks to her health and safety that were or should have been identified;
(b) the preventative and protective measures that were or should have been identified;
in breach of Regulation 8(1);

(v) Failed to discharge its duty under Regulation 11 in that they did not provide the Claimant with any or any adequate health and safety training;
(vi) Negligently failed to heed or act upon duties set out under the Health Regulations as set out above;

Management of Health & Safety Regulations 1999

1. Failed to make a suitable and sufficient assessment of the risks to health and safety of its employees whilst at work in breach of Regulation 3(1);

2. Failed to review the assessment set out above, in breach of Regulation 3(3);

3. Failed to record the significant findings of the assessment and any group of its employees identified by it as being especially at risk in breach of Regulation 3(6);

4. Failed to:
a. avoid the risks and/or
b. evaluate the risks which could be avoided;
c. combat the risks at source;
d. adapt the work to the individual as regards the choice of work equipment and the choice of working methods;
e. replace the dangerous or non-dangerous or less dangerous in breach of Regulation 4;
(f) develop and implement a coherent overall prevention policy which covered technology, organisation for work and working conditions.

5. Failed to make and give effect to appropriate measures for the effective planning, organisation, control, monitoring and review of the preventative and protective measures in breach of Regulation 5(1);

6. Failed to record the measures set out at sub-paragraph (xv) above in breach of Regulation 5(2);

7. Failed to ensure that the Claimant was provided with such health surveillance as appropriate in breach of Regulation 6;

8. Failed to provide the Claimant with information as to:
a. the risks to his health and safety identified by the assessment;
b. the preventative and protective measures to be taken;
in breach of Regulation 10(1);

9. Further and in the alternative to sub-paragraph (xxi) above, failed to repeat the training periodically and or to adapt the training to take into account new and/or changed risks to health and to have the training in working hours in breach of Regulation 13(3).

a. failed to make any or any suitable assessment of the risk created by requiring the Claimant to work in an environment where dust/ upvc particles were likely to be, and in fact were, present;
b. failed to make any or any suitable assessment of the steps to be taken to meet the requirements of the Regulations in breach of regulation 6(1) thereof;
c. failed to review regularly the assessment made negligently and/or in breach of regulation 6(2) of the Regulations;
d. failed to prevent the Claimant's exposure to any and/or all of the dust/ upvc particles set out in paragraph 3 above;
e. failed to provide any personal protective equipment negligently and/or in breach of regulation 7(5) of the Regulations and the Personal Protective Equipment at Work Regulations 1992/1999;
f. exposed the Claimant to levels of dust/ upvc particles set out in paragraph 3 above in excess of the maximum exposure limits negligently and/or in breach of regulation 7 of the Regulations;
g. failed to monitor exposure at the Claimant's workplace negligently and/or in breach of regulation 10 of the 1999 Regulations;
h. failed to devise or implement any or any adequate system of health surveillance negligently and/or in breach of regulation 11 of the 1999 Regulations;
i. failed to provide the Claimant with any or any adequate information, warning, instruction or training to enable her to know the risks to his health created by his exposure and the precautions to be taken negligently and/or in breach of regulation 12 of the Regulations;
j. failed to warn the Claimant to report any respiratory problems as soon as she became aware of them and/ or failed to take measures to abate such problems even when advised;
k. failed to heed or chose to ignore the information contained in Guidance note EH64 published by the Health and Safety Executive;
l. failed to heed or chose to ignore the recommendations set out in the Health and Safety Executive publication of 1994 – 'Preventing Asthma at work';
m. in the premises failed to provide the Claimant with a safe system of work.

Workplace (Health, Safety & Welfare) Regulations 1992

(i) In all the premises set out above, provided the Claimant with an unsafe place and system of work thereby exposing her to an unnecessary and unreasonable risk of injury.
Personal Protective Equipment at Work Regulations 1992 and 1999

(i) Failed to provide any or any adequate personal protective equipment negligently and/or in breach of regulation 7(5) of the Regulations and the Personal Protective Equipment at Work Regulations 1992/1999;

Control of Substances Hazardous to Health 1989, 1994, 1999 and 2002

(i) Failed to make a suitable and sufficient assessment of the risks created by the use of UPVC Particles ('the Substances') and of the steps which needed to be taken to meet the requirements of the Regulations and in particular failed to have regard to:
(ii) the hazardous properties of the Substances;
(iii) the information on health effects provided by the suppliers;
(iv) the level, type and duration of exposure;
(v) the circumstances of work including the amount of the substance involved;
(vi) activities such as cutting the material and installation, where there was the potential for a high level of exposure;
(vii) any relevant occupational exposure standard, maximum exposure limit or similar occupational exposure limit;
(viii) the effect of preventative or control measures;
(ix) the results of health surveillance;
(x) the results of monitoring exposure; in breach of regulation 6(1)
(xi) Failed to control the Claimant's exposure to the Substances or to control it adequately in breach of regulation 7(1);
(xii) Failed to eliminate or reduce the risk of exposure and/or use different substances and/or a different process to reduce the risk to the Claimant;
(xiii) Failed to comply with its duty of control by applying protection measures such as.

a. the design and use of appropriate work processes, systems and engineering controls and the provision of suitable work equipment and materials;
b. the control of exposure at source including adequate ventilation systems and organisational measures;
c. arrangements for the safe handling and storage of the Substances;
d. failed to totally enclose the processes involving the Substances;
e. failed to provide any or any suitable warnings signs relating to the substances; in breach of Regulation 6(5)
(xiv) Allowed or permitted the Claimant to inhale so much of the Substances that is was harmful in breach of Regulation 6(7);
(xv) Failed to provide the Claimant with any or any suitable personal protective equipment in breach of Regulation 6(9)
(xvi) Failed to ensure that any control measures were properly used or applied in breach of Regulation 9(1);
(xvii) Failed to monitor the exposure of the Claimant to the Substances contrary to Regulation 10(1) by means of a suitable procedure or otherwise;
(xviii) Failed to ensure that the Claimant was kept under suitable health surveillance, contrary to Regulation 11;
(xix) When health surveillance showed that the Claimant was found to have occupational asthma due to the exposure to the Substances failed to:
(a) review any risk assessments:
(b) review any other control measures;
(c) consider assigning the Claimant to alternative work until it was too late;
(xx) Failed to provide the Claimant with suitable and sufficient information, instruction and training including:
(a) the details of the Substances including the risk which they presented to health and any relevant occupation exposure limits and/or any similar limits and any legislative provisions which concern the hazardous properties of the Substances;
(b) the significant findings of any risk assessments;
(c) the appropriate precautions and actions to be taken by the Claimant in order to safeguard herself at the workplace;
(d) the results of any monitoring; in breach of Regulation 12

7. Further and/ or in the alternative, the Defendant were in breach of its common law duty of care to the Claimant in that they:-
a) Negligently failed to provide the building with appropriate ventilation, when they knew or ought to have known hazardous substances were being used;
b) Failed to warn the Claimant of the danger;
c) Failed to cease work on the site, even when it was clear it was presenting an exposure risk;
d) Failed to carry out any and/ or any adequate risk assessment;
e) Failed to move employees to a safe area of the building where employees would not be exposed to UPVC dust;
f) Failed to engage competent contractors and/ or employees to carry out the construction work;
g) Failed to provide any adequate training or instructions to employees, servants or agents undertaking the work;
h) Failed to seal off the area where the works were taking place, so as to prevent exposure;
i) Failed to carry out the works in such a time, place or manner, as to prevent exposure;
j) In the premises provided the Claimant with an unsafe place and system of work thereby exposing him to an unnecessary and unreasonable risk of injury;
k) Further and additionally, the Claimant relies on the happening of the accident itself as being proof of the Defendant's negligence and pleads res ipsa loquitur.

Example Cases – COSHH

OGDEN V AIREDALE HEALTH AUTHORITY (1996) - The defendant was negligent, and after 1988 in breach of statutory duty, in failing to take precautions to protect employees from hazards associated with chemicals used in the x-ray department. Damages included an award for loss of job security.

Another interesting case which looked at the law was **DARSHANA GLADWIN DASS v EASTERN & COASTAL KENT PRIMARY CARE TRUST (2013)** which led given the degree of risk, it had been sufficient for an employer to read the manufacturer's data sheets in order to assess the risks from ethanediol in paint used in the redecoration of a hospital. There had been no breach of the employer's statutory duty under the Control of Substances Regulation 7 of the Hazardous to Health Regulations.

In **YVONNE MARY NAYLOR V VOLEX GROUP PLC (SUED AS VOLEX WIRING SYSTEMS LTD) (2003)** the defendant employer was in breach of its statutory duty by failing to carry out a fresh assessment of the risks of exposure to colophony when it had knowledge that its previous method of risk assessment had been notified as unreliable. The Judgment said:-

> *Appellant, Mr.s.. Yvonne Naylor, was employed by the defendants, the Volex Group Plc, in work described more fully in the learned judge's judgment, but which for present purposes can be summarised as being the making-up of wiring harnesses for insertion into vans or other vehicles. Part of that operation involves the soldering of those wires. Mr.s.. Naylor was not originally directly involved in that.* ***Her case is that from April 1997 she was exposed to the actual soldering. That was in principle an operation exposing the employees to some hazard. The reason for that is set out in paragraph 4 of the learned judge's judgment, which I can do no better than to quote:***
>
> *".... in the soldering wire there was a rosin core and that rosin core, when it met the heat of the soldering iron, gave off a plume of what one would call smoke but which contains a substance called Colophony and those substances are hazardous to health."*
>
> ***The injury that Mr.s.. Naylor claimed to have suffered as a result of exposure to colophony was industrial asthma. There is a dispute as to the causation of that injury, which turns on a dispute as to when Mr.s.. Naylor ceased involvement in the work of soldering.*** *I shall have to return briefly at the end of the judgment to that question.*

The claim on which she succeeded at the trial was under the 1994 Control of Substances Hazardous to Health Regulations 1994 ("the regulations"). Regulations 6 and 7(1) provide as follows:

"6 Assessment of health risks created by work involving substances hazardous to health

(1) An employer shall not carry on any work which is liable to expose any employees to any substance hazardous to health unless he has made a suitable and sufficient assessment of the risks created by that work to the health of those employees and of the steps that need to be taken to meet the requirements of these Regulations.

(2) The assessment required by paragraph (1) shall be reviewed regularly and forthwith if -- (a) there is reason to suspect that the assessment is no longer valid; or

(b) there has been a significant change in the work to which the assessment relates,

and where, as a result of the review, changes in the assessment are required, those changes shall be made.

7 Prevention or control of exposure to substances hazardous to health

(1) Every employer shall ensure that the exposure of his employees to substances hazardous to health is either prevented or, where this is not reasonably practicable, adequately controlled."

When this appeal was initially put in hand and when permission was granted to appeal to this court, it was possible to say that there was some uncertainty about the state of authority in this court with regard to the true construction of those regulations; though I am bound to say that even at that stage that contention seemed to me to be a difficult one. ***However, the court now has the benefit of its recent decision in the case of Dugmore v Swansea NHS Trust [2002] EWCA Civ 1689. At this stage I need do no more than read paragraph 27 of the court's judgment, which is in the following terms:***

"This all reinforces the view taken by Lord Nimmo Smith [in Bilton v Fastnet Highlands [1998] SLT 1323] that the purpose of the regulations is protective and preventive: they do not rely simply on criminal sanctions or civil liability after the event to induce good practice. They involve positive obligations to seek out the risks and take precautions again them. It is by no means incompatible with their purpose that an employer who fails to discover a risk or rates it so low that he take no precautions against it should nevertheless be liable to the employee who suffers as a result."

The judgment of Lord Nimmo Smith, to which this court there refers, had compared the position under section 29(1) of the Factories Act 1961. Lord Nimmo Smith's view that that section also imposed a similar strict liability on the employer, comparable to that which he discerned in the regulations, echoed the general view of the relevance of the concept of reasonable praPctaicgae-bil2ityotfo7the employer's liability which was expressed by this court in Larner v British Steel [1993] 4 All ER 102. I would venture to mention in particular the citation by Hirst LJ at page 110D and by Peter Gibson J (as he then was) at page 113A of a dictum of Lord Guest in Nimmo v Alexander Cowan [1968] AC 122. I accept that those observations were addressed to a different provision, but it was clearly the view of Lord Nimmo Smith that they ran in parallel with the view that he took, and this court has now taken, of the present regulations.

I turn to this case.

It is common ground that colophony fumes have for many years been recognised as an environmental employment hazard. The question was what was the level, if any, of safe exposure to such fumes. Although the present employers provided general ventilation in the workplace, they had never provided local exhaust ventilation at the particular repair benches where the claimant's exposure occurred. Had such local exhaust ventilation been provided, as I understand it the problem would not have arisen.

Turning to the regulations, the judge found that there had been a breach of regulation 6 in circumstances to which I shall come, and also a breach of regulation 7. This he explained in paragraph 20 of his judgment. He first of all explains why he thought that in the circumstances a risk assessment had been required in January 1997 under the provisions of regulation 6(2)(a). (That finding of the judge is contested and I shall come back shortly to explain the basis upon which it was put.) He continued thus:

"It did not happen and so thereafter, in my judgment, (and I will come to the facts in a moment) if, in terms of breach of statutory duty, the employer breached 7(1) then, subject to the findings of fact which I will make further on, there has got to be liability ***in terms of a breach of statutory duty. I say that because there is no leeway in this statutory duty.*** *It is mandatory. 7(1) says:*

'Every employer shall ensure that the exposure of his employees to substances hazardous to health is either prevented or, where this is not reasonably practicable, adequately controlled.'

There has been no case advanced on behalf of the defendants in this court as far as I understand it as to prevention not being reasonably practicable in this factory and frankly I am not surprised because local exhaust ventilation ducts have been in this place for a very long time. ***They have just never been applied to the temporary repair benches. As a matter of law, I have come to the conclusion that any exposure after the .... 1st January [I will explain the importance of that date in a minute] would have and did amount to a breach of statutory duty in terms of 7(1)."***

I would respectfully comment that that approach seems to me to be exactly in line with the view subsequently taken by this court in Dugmore, that I have already set out.

I turn to the breaches in more detail.

First, the breach of regulation 6. The employers had originally, before 1997, made an assessment of risk, although we have not seen it and apparently it was not made in writing. That had led them to think that persons working in the situation of Mr.s. Naylor were not exposed to a significantly dangerous risk from colophony. That assessment was probably based upon standards provided by the Health and Safety Executive. In January 1997 the Health and Safety Executive standards were withdrawn. At broadly at the same time, the employers received a report from a firm of environmental consultants, to whom I will refer as RPS, with regard to exposure from colophony.

Evidence was given about the receipt of that report and other relevant matters by a Mr. Jones, who had been for many years the defendant's Group Health and Safety Officer and who was responsible for the defendant's reaction to health and safety hazards. The fact of withdrawal of the Health and Safety Executive requirements was set out in a leaflet produced by that body about which there was dispute as to when it had arrived in Mr. Jones' possession. He gave evidence to the judge, as I understand it, that he had had that leaflet in January 1997. The judge was later told (although Mr. Jones was not invited to go back into the witness box) that that had been an error on Mr. Jones' part. All that he had had in January was the RPS report. When the judge dealt with this matter in his judgment, it is fair to say -- and hardly surprising -- that he appears to have believed that Mr. Jones had the HSE report itself in January 1997. As I say, it is hardly surprising that he thought that in view of the evidence he had had to that effect.

I am content to deal with the matter, having been addressed at considerable length by Mr. Feeney on this point, on the basis that in truth all that the employerPhadgweas3thoefR7PS report at that date. If, however, one turns to that report, it is clear from it, and from passages that the judge cited, that there was serious cause for concern about the previous methods of testing. The consultants said this at page 2 of their report:

"Currently, the method by which colophony fume is sampled (and also the Occupational Exposure Standard) are under review by the HSE. This is because the above method for rosin core pyrolysis products only measures the gaseous components of the fume and there

is some doubt as to whether an OES based on formaldehyde exposure is appropriate ....

An alternative method for sampling colophony fume has been devised by the HSE to investigate the resin acids in solderfume that occur during rosin cored soldering. However, this method has not been fully verified and as yet no official occupational exposure standards have been set, so this method was not used in this survey."

On page 75 there is a table of limits but it is specifically noted as being in relation to substances under review by the Health and Safety Commission's Advisory Committee on Toxic Substances.

The judge said, believing that Mr. Jones had positive information that the HSE standard based upon the then Occupational Exposure Standards previously used had been actively withdrawn by the HSE, that that was a significant moment when it was necessary under section 6(2)(a) for there to be a reassessment, there being reason to suspect that the original assessment was no longer valid. That, if I may say so, was a clear and obvious conclusion from the evidence that was before him. But even if Mr. Jones had given evidence about his correct state of mind, that he only had the RPS report, nonetheless in my judgement that report itself should unambiguously have rung warning bells in the mind of any health and safety officer. What the employer was being told was that the sure standard previously relied on was under investigation, and could not safely be relied on. In those circumstances a finding that a new risk assessment was required, with the possible conclusion that the work either must be stopped or that the practicable step of installing local ventilation should be taken, was clearly something that should have come to attention.

I say all that because it appears to be suggested in this appeal that, because of the confusion about which document Mr. Jones actually had in January, this appeal should be allowed to the extent of the matter being remitted to the learned judge for him to review the regulation 6 position on the basis solely of the RPS report. That in my judgement would be a futile exercise because even if that were done, it would certainly be open to the judge -- and I would go so far as to say he might well be bound -- to find that the reliance on the RPS document alone led him inexorably to the same conclusion. There are no grounds, therefore, for going behind the judge's finding as to regulation 6. I have gone into that matter at some length because of the complaint that was made about the confusion as to the underlying documents.

The question as to breach of regulation 7 is somewhat more straightforward. The judge is criticised because he said, in the passage that I have already read, that there was no claim made in respect of reasonable practicability. He is said to have misunderstood paragraph 4 of the defence, which reads as follows:

"In the circumstances, the Claimant's exposure to colophony fumes was minimal. At the material time there was no official standard for colophony exposure. The previous Occupational Exposure Standard had been withdrawn by the Health & Safety Executive and a new Maximum Exposure Limit was proposed. However, the Defendants deny that the Claimant's exposure was such as to exceed the previous OES or the proposed MEL. The Defendants deny that they could reasonably have anticipated in the light of contemporaneous knowledge that the Claimant would have suffered any injury as a result of her minimal exposure to colophony fumes."

I am not surprised, in the light of that pleading, that the judge did not understand what the pleader apparently was seeking to say to him. No word is said in that pleading about reasonable practicability. What is relied on is lack of knowledge or foresight and that, first of all, is a different matter from reasonable practicability; and, secondly, under these regulations properly construed, is not a consideration that can be taken into account.

The judge said this about paragraph 4 in paragraph 21 of his judgment:

".... whilst the contents of paragraph 4 are very interesting and probably inform the court as to why the decision was taken to defend the action .... it does not, in my judgment, amount to any, or any adequate, response to a plain breach of section 7. If there is exposure,

it does not matter how minimal. Regulation says that there is to be no exposure."

That was directly in line, in my judgement, with the view taken by this court in Dugmore. Mr. Feeney sought to distinguish Dugmore in a number of respects. I am not persuaded by any of them. In my judgement, first of all what this court said in Dugmore was of general application; and, secondly, there is no feature in this case that renders the employer's position more favourable than that of the employer in Dugmore. In any event, as the judge himself said, if there had been a breach of regulation 6 by not getting the proper information and not putting themselves in the right position that they should have been in, then even if ignorance or lack of foresight was a potentially available plea under regulation 7 it cannot be available in a case where the employer is in the state of knowledge that he is in because he has not performed his duty under regulation 6.

On the main question of liability, therefore, this appeal is in my judgement bound to fail.

I come to the two factual questions. The first concerns the dates at which Mr.s.. Naylor was exposed to colophony. On the medical evidence it was common ground that the diagnosis of occupational asthma on which the claim depended needed the claimant to show that she had worked on soldering in July to October 1997 on her return to work from her honeymoon, as well as during a previous period in April to May of 1997. At the trial, but not before, the claimant advanced circumstantial considerations to support her evidence of that fact, saying that she had gone back to soldering because of the removal of a fellow worker, a Mr.s. Hatton, to another section of the factory when she, Mr.s. Hatton, also returned from honeymoon. Mr.s. Hatton was already a witness as to the general nature of soldering, but she only volunteered evidence supporting that aspect of Mr.s. Naylor's claim at the trial itself. The defendants had called a witness, a Mr.s. Farrimond, to say that Mr.s. Hatton had only transferred to the other work in 1998. That evidence was given, as we understand it, on the second day of the trial, Mr.s. Farrimond saying that she had consulted the wage records from 1998 which established Mr.s. Hatton's position in 1998. It was pointed out that those records did not cover the relevant period of 1997. Therefore there were produced overnight, and after Mr.s. Naylor and Mr.s. Hatton had completed their evidence, the wage slips for Mr.s. Hatton which were said to demonstrate that there had been no such increase in her pay over the relevant period in 1997 as would have been granted for the new job to which she said she had moved.

The judge understood the employer's case on this point to be -- and we have not been told by Mr. Feeney otherwise -- that Mr.s. Naylor was not just mistaken about the period of her employment but was activity lying about it. He dealt with that allegation in the light of the wage slips in this way (paragraph 31):

"The point that Mr.s. Farrimond was taking is that there would have been extra pay in the job that Denise Hatton said she went off to do and she checked the records for 1998. She did not, unfortunately, check the records for 1997, which is the year in question, so that was not at all helpful. I am told the defendants endeavoured to produce her wage slips because they would have reflected the increase[d] pay but there are only four wage slips for the week of 1st August, 5th September, 12th and 19th September. That is all.

Do I accept from Mr.s. Farrimond her trenchant assertions that the claimant's account is not true and Denise Hatton cannot be right because the records do not show extra pay? I do not find Mr.s. Farrimond that reliable to reach those conclusions. Using my common sense as a Judge, looking at milestone events in people's lives, I am very impressed by the coincidence that these two ladies had honeymoons within a very short period of each other and that that was a significant milestone event in both their lives. It gave them a good reference point for their recollections."

He therefore found, in the face of strong allegations against them, that both of those witnesses were telling the truth; and of course he had seen and heard them give evidence.

Before us there is an application in terms of the jurisprudence of Ladd Marshall [1954] 1 WLR 1489 to admit not only the four wage slips that were at the trial but also a significant number of further wage slips which are said to demonstrate that Mr.s. Hatton did not move until 1998. That is supported by a substantial witness statement by Mr. Simon Denyer, the solicitor for the appellants. The difficulty about that application, it seems to me, is this. There were already present at the trial, albeit belatedly, wage slips available to be used, if so interpreted, to challenge the evidence of Mr.s. Hatton. Indeed, in paragraph 8 of his witness statement in support of this application, Mr. Denyer points out that one of those wage slips was, as he puts it. "crucial for causation", because it covered a particular month in 1997 in respect of which month both the claimant and Mr.s. Hatton had suggested that Mr.s. Hatton had already moved. There was, therefore, relevant evidence in this sense already before the court. As we understand it, those slips were produced but no further application was made either for an adjournment or to recall certainly Mr.s. Naylor and possibly Mr.s. Hatton, and to confront them with these slips.

One understands why it was thought best to take that course. Applications for recalling witnesses or, much worse, for adjourning the trial are not lightly made. The fact remains, however, that this court has to decide whether it should now allow this appeal to the extent of sending the matter back to the judge for further consideration. On the evidence supporting the application, which I have already set out, it is difficult to see how the new slips covering 1998 will improve the position as it was originally before the judge. The substance of this complaint therefore is not really that there was new evidence that ought to have been before the judge, but that he made an inadmissible or improper assessment of the evidence that he actually had: which did include, at the end of the day, these wage slips. It seems to me impossible to say that the course that the judge took was not open to him. He was faced with two witnesses whom he had heard give evidence, who had not been confronted with the slips although they could have been, and whom he clearly found to be witnesses of truth. In my judgement it would be quite inappropriate now to send the matter back to the judge effectively suggesting that he ought to think again. I would therefore not grant the application and would not allow the appeal on that point.

Finally, complaint is made about the judge's treatment of the medical evidence. It was a strong point put against Mr.s. Naylor that she had been suffering from conventional (as I will call it) asthma before coming into contact with colophony, and therefore her asthmatic symptoms of which she complained, and which were established, were not causally related to the colophony. Reliance was placed upon a number of doctors' notes that suggested breathing difficulties in the early days of 1997. Reliance was also placed on a note taken at Bolton Metropolitan Hospital when Mr.s. Naylor presented there in a condition of considerable distress with her breathing in October 1997, which reported a history given by her husband that she had suffered breathing problems for some undefined period prior to that, but certainly predating the exposure to colophony"

The judge had the benefit of very skilled medical evidence, including the evidence on behalf of the claimant of a Dr Rudd, who is a most distinguished consultant in this field. ***Dr Rudd had had the benefit of not only examining the claimant but also taking a history from her and her husband. Mr. Naylor's evidence at the trial was that his wife had not had previous respiratory problems, and I will note in passing that the judge specifically recorded that Mr. Naylor was a witness of truth. Dr Rudd, being shown the notes, gave what I have to say is a comprehensive account of them to the judge. He expressed the view that the earliest of them did not record asthma but upper respiratory tract infection, and the General Practitioner had never suggested otherwise; and that the note that emanated from the visit to Bolton Hospital could not be relied upon.*** *It was a houseman's note taken at a time of considerable stress for all concerned, and was the sort of note that would not be relied upon against the presence of other evidence. That is, if I may say so, exactly the sort of informed judgment of a medical history that an experienced clinician is entitled to make, and it is exactly the sort of evidence that a judge in his turn is entitled to accept, if he finds it convincing, from a man of that standing in the profession. The notes themselves, of course, prove nothing. They require to be interpreted. In this case each and every one of them, in my judgement, was as a whole interpreted by Dr Rudd in a sense that the judge was entitled to accept. There are no reasons for seeking to go behind the medical* *findings in this case and I am bound to say that I have to express some surprise that that was even attempted".*

Quantum

Many cases of COSHH are related to asthma / respiratory complaints. Please refer to the relevant section of the 14th edition of the Judicial College Guidelines.

Summary of COSHH

1. It will be important to identify how the exposure is hazardous within the meaning of the Regulations.

2. The expert must link causation to the exposure/ breach. For example, on industrial asthma the Claimant may require a respiratory expert in this respect.

3. It must be shown, on balance, that the employer must have known or reasonably ought to have known there was a risk, in order to succeed in these cases.

4. The risk assessment that the Defendant conducted as to potential exposure is essential – does that deal with minimising risk from hazardous materials and is the risk assessment updated?

The HSE website says:-

Regulation 6 - Risk assessment

11 Regulation 6(1)(a) requires that employers should not carry out work that is liable to expose employees to substances hazardous to health until all risks have been evaluated and minimised as set down in the regulations. COSHH 2002 regulation 6(1)(b) introduces a further requirement to implement the steps highlighted in the assessment before commencing any work liable to expose employees to any relevant hazardous substance(s).

12 Regulation 6(2) of COSHH 2002 (as amended), now provides a list of issues which employers should include and consider for their assessment to be deemed suitable and sufficient. This includes a requirement to consider the information provided by the supplier, including that given in safety data sheets (SDSs), when making their assessment. SDSs are a valuable source of information but inspectors and enforcement officers should be aware that a significant proportion contains inaccuracies. The ACOP 'The compilation of Safety Data Sheets' third edition (L130) is of relevance here. If employers have concerns about the accuracy of this information e.g. misclassification of a hazard or omission of a well known health effect, inspectors and enforcement officers should encourage them to raise this with their suppliers. Where such inaccuracies are serious, especially if these could lead to exposure to substances causing a serious health effect, then inspectors and enforcement officers should consider enforcement action against the supplier under the Chemicals (Hazard Information and Packaging for Supply) Regulations 2002 (to be replaced by the requirements of the Regulation Evaluation Authority and restriction of Chemicals, or REACH, between 2008-2018).

13 In view of the emphasis placed by regulation 7(2) on preventing exposure by substituting the hazardous substance or process in order to eliminate or reduce the risk, inspectors and enforcement officers should check that the employer has recorded the extent to which prevention and substitution have been considered.

CHAPTER NINE

REPETITIVE STRAIN CASES / UPPER LIMB CASES INCLUDING CARPAL TUNNEL SYNDROME ('CTS') CASES – BREACH OF DUTY CAUSATION AND QUANTUM

Manual Handling Accidents – the Manual Handling Operations Regulations 1992, Key Cases and Proving Negligence

The Regulations set out as follows:-

> ***Duties of employers***
>
> *4.—(1) Each employer shall—*
>
> *(a) so far as is reasonably practicable, avoid the need for his employees to undertake any manual handling operations at work which involve a risk of their being injured; or*
>
> *(b) where it is not reasonably practicable to avoid the need for his employees to undertake any manual handling operations at work which involve a risk of their being injured—*
>
> *(i) make a suitable and sufficient assessment of all such manual handling operations to be undertaken by them, having regard to the factors which are specified in column 1 of Schedule 1 to these Regulations and considering the questions which are specified in the corresponding entry in column 2 of that Schedule,*
>
> *(ii) take appropriate steps to reduce the risk of injury to those employees arising out of their undertaking any such manual handling operations to the lowest level reasonably practicable, and*

(iii) take appropriate steps to provide any of those employees who are undertaking any such manual handling operations with general indications and, where it is reasonably practicable to do so, precise information on—

(aa) the weight of each load, and

(bb) the heaviest side of any load whose centre of gravity is not positioned centrally.

(2) Any assessment such as is referred to in paragraph (1)(b)(i) of this regulation shall be reviewed by the employer who made it if—

(a) there is reason to suspect that it is no longer valid; or

(b) there has been a significant change in the manual handling operations to which it relates;

and where as a result of any such review changes to an assessment are required, the relevant employer shall make them.

Duty of employees

5. Each employee while at work shall make full and proper use of any system of work provided for his use by his employer in compliance with regulation 4(1)(b)(ii) of these Regulations.

SCHEDULE 1

FACTORS TO WHICH THE EMPLOYER MUST HAVE REGARD AND QUESTIONS HE MUST CONSIDER WHEN MAKING AN ASSESSMENT OF MANUAL HANDLING OPERATIONS

Factors	*Questions*
1. The tasks	***Do they involve:*** *holding or manipulating loads at distance from trunk?* *unsatisfactory bodily movement or posture* *twisting the trunk?* *stooping?* *reaching upwards?* *excessive movement of loads, especially:* *excessive lifting or lowering distances?* *excessive carrying distances?* *excessive pushing or pulling of loads?* *risk of sudden movement of loads?* *frequent or prolonged physical effort?* *insufficient rest or recovery periods?* *a rate of work imposed by a process?*
2. The loads	***Are they:*** *heavy?* *bulky or unwieldy?* *difficult to grasp?* *unstable, or with contents likely to shift?* *sharp, hot or otherwise potentially damaging?*
3. The working environment	***Are there:*** *space constraints preventing good posture?* *uneven, slippery or unstable floors?* *variations in level of floors or work surfaces?* *extremes of temperature or humidity?* *conditions causing ventilation problems or gusts of wind?* *poor lighting conditions?*
4. Individual capability	***Does the job:*** *require unusual strength, height, etc.?* *create a hazard to those who might reasonably be considered* *to be pregnant or to have a health problem?* *require special information or training for its safe performance?*
5. Other factors	***Is movement or posture hindered by personal protective equipment or by clothing?***

The Health and Safety (Miscellaneous Amendments) Regulations 2002 provide:

> "*Amendment of the Manual Handling Operations Regulations 1992*
> *4. Regulation 4 of the Manual Handling Operations Regulations 1992 shall be amended by adding the following paragraph—*
>
> *"(3) In determining for the purposes of this regulation whether manual handling operations at work involve a risk of injury and in determining the appropriate steps to reduce that risk regard shall be had in particular to—*
> *(a) the physical suitability of the employee to carry out the operations;*
> *(b) the clothing, footwear or other personal effects he is wearing;*
> *(c) his knowledge and training;*
> *(d) the results of any relevant risk assessment carried out pursuant to regulation 3 of the Management of Health and Safety at Work Regulations 1999;*
> *(e) whether the employee is within a group of employees identified by that assessment as being especially at risk; and*
> *(f) the results of any health surveillance provided pursuant to regulation 6 of the Management of Health and Safety Regulations 1999."*

A Case in Point – Manual Handling

The following are examples of cases that failed under the HM Regulations. In **SHAUN NAREY v ICELAND FOODS LTD (2015)** the facts were as follows from the Judgment:-

> "*2. On 23 July 2011 the claimant, whilst carrying a plastic crate of shopping, including tins of dog food, for home delivery, lost his grip on the crate resulting in it falling on his right big toe with resulting injuries including a crush injury to the distal phalanx of his right big toe, a compound fracture.*
>
> *3. The claimant says that the defendant failed to provide personal protective equipment to him in the form of steel toe capped boots and was therefore in breach of the Manual Handling Regulations and*

Personal Protective Equipment at Work Regulations. The defendant admits injury occurred as a result of the accident and that it did not provide the claimant with protective footwear"

The Law

> "*The burden of proving that the defendant has complied with the relevant regulations falls on the defendant. The defendant relies on the regulations set out above. The standard of proof is the civil standard on a balance of probabilities".*
> [It should however be noted that post ERRA this would no longer be the case].

The Defendant argued that:-

> "*28. The defendant submits it fulfilled its duty under regulation 4(1)(b)(i) because it was not reasonably practicable to avoid the need for the claimant to carry out the manual handling operation and a risk assessment of the operation had been carried out.*
>
> *29. In relation to regulation 4(l)(b)(ii) the defendant said it fulfilled its duty because it had reduced the risk to the lowest level reasonably practicable with the provision of suitable and safe equipment, training and instruction"*

The Court found:-

> ***36. I am satisfied that the risk assessment carried out was a "suitable and sufficient assessment of the identified risk to employees in handling the home delivery crates.*** *A maximum weight was imposed. Whilst the employees may not have had specific training on assessing weight I take into account that the loads were bags of shopping which could be seen as to content and about which any person could form a view as to weight and they had examples of weight every day. I do not consider that additional training on assessing weight would assist. Each load will be quite different. It would not be practical to weigh each load as that in itself would*

necessitate further lifting and handling. There is also another check in that the crates could not be overloaded as they would not then stack and this was part of training.

37. The crates may have been unstable the claimant suggests when one is balanced on another and it is moved with the weight supported. The claimant was shown how to do this. I accept the evidence of Mr. Stevens that it is unlikely the contents would move to the extent that the there was a risk the crate would be dropped. ***In any event such a risk had been assessed and training provided.*** *There were 2 sturdy grips on each crate, one for each hand to stabilise the crate during such an operation.*

38. Whilst access to top crates may be assessed as a high risk, there is a policy that the stacks are not more than 5 crates high and only 4 if being moved. An ***employee has a duty to keep himself safe and a shorter person could have problem, in which case he or she must seek help.*** *That is part of the training.*

39. After consideration of all the evidence, I consider that the risk assessments undertaken are suitable and sufficient and that the training put in place addresses those risks in accordance with Regulation 4(1)(b)(ii) The Manual Handling Operations Regulations 1992.

40. The claimant's claim therefore fails on breach of statutory duty.

Points to Note

1. Manual Handling cases are often going to focus on the issue of risk assessments and training.
2. Consider in detail the defendant's risk assessments for Manual Handling at an early stage, together with training records. If the claimant had been trained in Manual Handling techniques but not adopted the techniques and the risk assessments had addressed the risk, then the case is likely to fail.

3. The stronger manual handling cases are likely to be those where there are no adequate risk assessments, or no risk assessments are all, or the claimant has received no manual handling training.

4. However, be aware of generic manual handling risk assessments, it is arguable that the risk assessments must address the specific task in question.

5. Remember that post ERRA cases, proof of negligence will be required, but the 1992 Regulations will be a good guide as to the standard of care, and thus the Regulations should always be pleaded.

6. The medical expert must link causation of injury to breach of duty i.e. the injury was caused by manual handling.

7. The Court is likely to focus upon what steps the defendant took to reduce the risk of manual handling activities to the lowest possible level. For example, could equipment have been provided to reduce a repetitive activity?

Accident involving Work Equipment - The Provision and Use of Work Equipment Regulations 1998, Key Cases and Proving Negligence

There are a number of relevant Regulations that can be pleaded and utilised in pre-section 69 ERRA 2013 cases (see earlier Chapters regarding the Enterprise Act).

Application of the 1998 Work Equipment Regulations

3.—(1) These Regulations shall apply—
(a) in Great Britain; and
(b) outside Great Britain as sections 1 to 59 and 80 to 82 of the 1974 Act apply by virtue of the Health and Safety at Work etc. Act 1974 (Application outside Great Britain) Order 1995(1) ("the 1995 Order").

(2) The requirements imposed by these Regulations on an employer in respect of work equipment shall apply to such equipment provided for use or used by an employee of his at work.

(3) The requirements imposed by these Regulations on an employer shall also apply—
(a) to a self-employed person, in respect of work equipment he uses at work;
(b) subject to paragraph (5), to a person who has control to any extent of—
(i) work equipment;
(ii) a person at work who uses or supervises or manages the use of work equipment; or
(iii) the way in which work equipment is used at work,
and to the extent of his control.

(4) Any reference in paragraph (3)(b) to a person having control is a reference to a person having control in connection with the carrying on by him of a trade, business or other undertaking (whether for profit or not).

Common Citations

The most commonly cited Regulations relate to suitability, maintenance and inspection, of Work Equipment, which are as follows:-

Suitability of work equipment

4.—(1) Every employer shall ensure that work equipment is so constructed or adapted as to be suitable for the purpose for which it is used or provided.

(2) In selecting work equipment, every employer shall have regard to the working conditions and to the risks to the health and safety of persons which exist in the premises or undertaking in which that work equipment is to be used and any additional risk posed by the use of that work equipment.

(3) Every employer shall ensure that work equipment is used only for operations for which, and under conditions for which, it is suitable.

(4) In this regulation "suitable" means suitable in any respect which it is reasonably foreseeable will affect the health or safety of any person.

Maintenance

5.—(1) Every employer shall ensure that work equipment is maintained in an efficient state, in efficient working order and in good repair.

(2) Every employer shall ensure that where any machinery has a maintenance log, the log is kept up to date.

Inspection

6.—(1) Every employer shall ensure that, where the safety of work equipment depends on the installation conditions, it is inspected—
(a) after installation and before being put into service for the first time; or
(b) after assembly at a new site or in a new location,
to ensure that it has been installed correctly and is safe to operate.

(2) Every employer shall ensure that work equipment exposed to conditions causing deterioration which is liable to result in dangerous situations is inspected—
(a) at suitable intervals; and
(b) each time that exceptional circumstances which are liable to jeopardise the safety of the work equipment have occurred,
to ensure that health and safety conditions are maintained and that any deterioration can be detected and remedied in good time.

(3) Every employer shall ensure that the result of an inspection made under this regulation is recorded and kept until the next inspection under this regulation is recorded.

(4) Every employer shall ensure that no work equipment—
(a) leaves his undertaking; or
(b) if obtained from the undertaking of another person, is used in his undertaking,
unless it is accompanied by physical evidence that the last inspection required to be carried out under this regulation has been carried out.

(5) This regulation does not apply to—
(a) a power press to which regulations 32 to 35 apply;
(b) a guard or protection device for the tools of such power press;
(c) work equipment for lifting loads including persons;
(d) winding apparatus to which the Mines (Shafts and Winding) Regulations 1993(1) apply;
(e) work equipment required to be inspected by regulation 29 of the Construction (Health, Safety and Welfare) Regulations 1996(2).

HSE Guidance – Maintenance, Inspection and Suitability

The HSE guidance which can be found at: http://www.hse.gov.uk/pubns/indg291.pdf, also provides the following useful guidance to the applicability of the Regulations:-

You must ensure that the work equipment you provide meets the requirements of PUWER. You should ensure that it is:

• suitable for use, and for the purpose and conditions in which it is to be used;

• maintained in a safe condition for use so that people's health and safety is not at risk; and

• inspected, in certain circumstances, to ensure that it is and continues to be safe for use. Any inspection should be carried out by a competent person (this could be an employee if they have the necessary skills, knowledge and experience to perform the task) and a record kept until the next inspection.

You should also ensure that risks created by using the equipment are eliminated where possible or controlled as far as reasonably practicable by:

- *taking appropriate 'hardware' measures, eg providing suitable guards, protection devices, markings and warning devices, system control devices (such as emergency stop buttons) and personal protective equipment; and*

- *taking appropriate 'software' measures such as following safe systems of work (eg ensuring maintenance is only performed when equipment is shut down etc), and providing adequate information, instruction and training about the specific equipment.*

A combination of these measures may be necessary depending on the requirements of the work, your assessment of the risks involved, and the practicability of such measures.

The Main Case – Stark v Post Office

The main case of Stark sets out as follows, to show how in relation to pre-Enterprise Act cases, the Regulations would impose strict liability in relation to defective work equipment cases:-

Mr. Stark the appellant is 60 years of age. He was employed as a delivery postman by the Post Office the respondents. The Post Office provided him with a bicycle with which to make his deliveries. On 29th July 1994 in the course of his employment he was riding his bicycle along Padstow Close, Bransholme, Hull when without warning his front wheel locked and he was propelled over the handlebars and suffered serious injury. The accident was caused by the fact that the stirrup, part of the front brake, broke in two, and one part lodged in the front wheel.

The Post Office did in fact have a policy of replacing bicycles at 10 years, but this was not an inflexible rule. Sometimes, (as in the case of this bicycle) they thought this bicycle had a few years serviceable life left and allowed it to continue in service. This bicycle was in its 14th year. The judge found that if it had been replaced at 10 years the accident would have been prevented but did not suggest there was any fault on the part of the Post Office in taking the decision they did.

In the result His Honour Judge Cracknell found that there was no liability in negligence and from that finding there is no appeal.

The judge also found that there was no breach of statutory duty, and thus dismissed Mr. Stark's claim. The regulations relied on by Mr. Wood on behalf of Mr. Stark before the judge were regulations 5 and 6 of the Provision and Use of Work Equipment Regulations 1992. Before us .r Redfern QC has not relied on regulation 5 and this appeal is concerned with the judge's ruling that regulation 6(1) was not breached by the Post Office. Regulation 6(1) is in the following terms:-

"Every employer shall ensure that work equipment is maintained in an efficient state, in efficient working order and in good repair."

It seems that the argument before the judge on behalf of the Post Office was that the regulation did not apply because the regulation was concerned with maintenance and not with replacement, and that if anything this was a replacement case. I am not sure the judge accepted that argument because at page 3 of his judgment he said:-

"On the face of the matter therefore it seems that this regulation may import strict liability into this part of the law. On the other hand, it seems to me the primary obligation is to institute and carry out a system of maintenance to the very best of their ability and this the Post Office did. At the risk of indulging in sophistry the visible state of the bicycle immediately prior to the event would have confirmed that fact."

Mr. Redfern's argument is that regulation 6(1) imposes an absolute obligation. His argument is straightforward. Work equipment is defined as "any machinery, appliance, apparatus or tool and any assembly of components which, in order to achieve a common end, are arranged and controlled so that they function as a whole" (see regulation 2(1)). That definition includes a bicycle but may place some limit on Mr. Storey's suggested "all-embracing". He submitted that "maintained in an efficient state, in efficient working order . . . " meant that the bicycle had to be kept in a state in which it worked efficiently at all times; the bicycle was not working efficiently when the stirrup broke; and that whatever the reason for it not working efficiently, the Post Office were in breach of the regulation.

He submitted that the wording used in regulation 6(1) had been construed as imposing such an absolute obligation when used in other regulations concerned with the safety of employees. He relied in particular on Galashiels Gas Co Ltd v Millar [1949] AC 275 and Hamilton v National Coal Board [1960] AC 633. In Galashiels the headnote reads:-

"By the Factories Act, 1937, s. 22, sub-s. 1: "Every hoist or lift shall be of good mechanical construction, sound material and adequate strength, and be -3- properly maintained." By s. 152, sub-s. 1, the expression "maintained" means "maintained in an efficient state, in efficient working order and in good repair."

By s. 22, sub-s. 1, an absolute and continuing obligation is imposed, so that proof of any failure in the mechanism of a hoist or lift establishes a breach of the statutory duty, even though it was impossible to anticipate that failure before the event or to explain it afterwards and even though all reasonable steps have been taken to provide a suitable hoist or lift and to maintain it properly."

The Court concluded:-

The draftsman here has used language construed as imposing a strict obligation over many years in the context of the Health and Safety of employees. That language gives effect to the minimum obligations, but it also goes further. I cannot see that there is any discouragement of the implementation of a higher standard if the Member State chooses to impose it.

In the circumstances it seems to me that regulation 6(1) does impose an absolute obligation, and that accordingly since the bicycle was not in an efficient state or in efficient working order when the stirrup broke, the Post Office were in breach of their statutory duty.

In those circumstances I would allow the appeal and enter judgment for Mr. Stark with damages to be assessed.

Other Essential Components of the 1998 Regulations

Specific risks

7.—(1) Where the use of work equipment is likely to involve a specific risk to health or safety, every employer shall ensure that—
(a) the use of that work equipment is restricted to those persons given the task of using it; and
(b) repairs, modifications, maintenance or servicing of that work equipment is restricted to those persons who have been specifically designated to perform operations of that description (whether or not also authorised to perform other operations).

(2) The employer shall ensure that the persons designated for the purposes of sub-paragraph (b) of paragraph (1) have received adequate training related to any operations in respect of which they have been so designated.

Information and instructions

8.—(1) Every employer shall ensure that all persons who use work equipment have available to them adequate health and safety information and, where appropriate, written instructions pertaining to the use of the work equipment.

(2) Every employer shall ensure that any of his employees who supervises or manages the use of work equipment has available to him adequate health and safety information and, where appropriate, written instructions pertaining to the use of the work equipment.

(3) Without prejudice to the generality of paragraphs (1) or (2), the information and instructions required by either of those paragraphs shall include information and, where appropriate, written instructions on—
(a) the conditions in which and the methods by which the work equipment may be used;
(b) foreseeable abnormal situations and the action to be taken if such a situation were to occur; and
(c) any conclusions to be drawn from experience in using the work equipment.
(4) Information and instructions required by this regulation shall be readily comprehensible to those concerned.

Training

9.—(1) Every employer shall ensure that all persons who use work equipment have received adequate training for purposes of health and safety, including training in the methods which may be adopted when using the work equipment, any risks which such use may entail and precautions to be taken.

(2) Every employer shall ensure that any of his employees who supervises or manages the use of work equipment has received adequate training for purposes of health and safety, including training in the methods which may be adopted when using the work equipment, any risks which such use may entail and precautions to be taken.

Dangerous parts of machinery

11.—(1) Every employer shall ensure that measures are taken in accordance with paragraph (2) which are effective—
(a) to prevent access to any dangerous part of machinery or to any rotating stock-bar; or
(b) to stop the movement of any dangerous part of machinery or rotating stock-bar before any part of a person enters a danger zone.

(2) The measures required by paragraph (1) shall consist of—

(a) the provision of fixed guards enclosing every dangerous part or rotating stock-bar where and to the extent that it is practicable to do so, but where or to the extent that it is not, then
(b) the provision of other guards or protection devices where and to the extent that it is practicable to do so, but where or to the extent that it is not, then
(c) the provision of jigs, holders, push-sticks or similar protection appliances used in conjunction with the machinery where and to the extent that it is practicable to do so, but where or to the extent that it is not, then
(d) the provision of information, instruction, training and supervision.

(3) All guards and protection devices provided under sub-paragraphs (a) or (b) of paragraph (2) shall—
(a) be suitable for the purpose for which they are provided;
(b) be of good construction, sound material and adequate strength;
(c) be maintained in an efficient state, in efficient working order and in good repair;
(d) not give rise to any increased risk to health or safety;
(e) not be easily bypassed or disabled;
(f) be situated at sufficient distance from the danger zone;
(g) not unduly restrict the view of the operating cycle of the machinery, where such a view is necessary;
(h) be so constructed or adapted that they allow operations necessary to fit or replace parts and for maintenance work, restricting access so that it is allowed only to the area where the work is to be carried out and, if possible, without having to dismantle the guard or protection device.

(4) All protection appliances provided under sub-paragraph (c) of paragraph (2) shall comply with sub-paragraphs (a) to (d) and (g) of paragraph (3).

(5) In this regulation—
"danger zone" means any zone in or around machinery in which a person is exposed to a risk to health or safety from contact with a dangerous part of machinery or a rotating stock-bar;

"stock-bar" means any part of a stock-bar which projects beyond the head-stock of a lathe.

Protection against specified hazards

12.—(1) Every employer shall take measures to ensure that the exposure of a person using work equipment to any risk to his health or safety from any hazard specified in paragraph (3) is either prevented, or, where that is not reasonably practicable, adequately controlled.

(2) The measures required by paragraph (1) shall—
(a) be measures other than the provision of personal protective equipment or of information, instruction, training and supervision, so far as is reasonably practicable; and
(b) include, where appropriate, measures to minimise the effects of the hazard as well as to reduce the likelihood of the hazard occurring.

(3) The hazards referred to in paragraph (1) are—
(a) any article or substance falling or being ejected from work equipment;
(b) rupture or disintegration of parts of work equipment;
(c) work equipment catching fire or overheating;
(d) the unintended or premature discharge of any article or of any gas, dust, liquid, vapour or other substance which, in each case, is produced, used or stored in the work equipment;
(e) the unintended or premature explosion of the work equipment or any article or substance produced, used or stored in it.

(4) For the purposes of this regulation "adequately" means adequately having regard only to the nature of the hazard and the nature and degree of exposure to the risk.

(5) This regulation shall not apply where any of the following Regulations apply in respect of any risk to a person's health or safety for which such Regulations require measures to be taken to prevent or control such risk, namely—
(a) the Ionising Radiations Regulations 1985(1);

(b) the Control of Asbestos at Work Regulations 1987(2);
(c) the Control of Substances Hazardous to Health Regulations 1994(3);
(d) the Noise at Work Regulations 1989(4);
(e) the Construction (Head Protection) Regulations 1989(5);
(f) the Control of Lead at Work Regulations 1998(6).

Controls for starting or making a significant change in operating conditions

14.—(1) Every employer shall ensure that, where appropriate, work equipment is provided with one or more controls for the purposes of —

(a) starting the work equipment (including re-starting after a stoppage for any reason); or
(b) controlling any change in the speed, pressure or other operating conditions of the work equipment where such conditions after the change result in risk to health and safety which is greater than or of a different nature from such risks before the change.

(2) Subject to paragraph (3), every employer shall ensure that, where a control is required by paragraph (1), it shall not be possible to perform any operation mentioned in sub-paragraph (a) or (b) of that paragraph except by a deliberate action on such control.

(3) Paragraph (1) shall not apply to re-starting or changing operating conditions as a result of the normal operating cycle of an automatic device.

Investigating Work Equipment Regulations Cases Post ERRA

It is always worth remembering that for Post ERR Act cases, the Claimant Lawyer will need to prove negligence. Some key points to consider are:-

1. Even though the 1998 Regulation no longer impose strict liability, it is still useful to plead the relevant Regulations for post

ERRA cases, as they are a useful guide as to the likely standards of care.

2. Disease cases are likely to focus on the failure to provide suitable work equipment rather than a failure of the equipment.

Work Related Upper Limb Disorders – Other Potential Regulations

- Personal Protective Equipment Regulations
- Management of Health & Safety Regulations 1999, ('the Safety Regulations').

Repetitive Strain Case – Example Breach of Duty

Example RSI caused by repetitive work in a bottle factory.

1. Manual Handling Operations Regulation 1992

a. *Negligently and/or in breach of Regulation 4(1)(a), caused the Claimant to undertake a manual handling operation namely lifting bottles and printing labels onto bottles, and failed to act upon the Claimant's complaints and / or make reasonable adjustments and / or failed to so far as is reasonably practicable, avoid the need for the Claimant to undertake any manual handling operations at work which involve a risk of their being injured*
b. *Negligently and/or in breach of Regulation 4(1)(b), failed to make a suitable and sufficient assessment of the task of lifting bottles and putting labels onto bottles particular, failed to have regard to the following:*
i. The task involved unsatisfactory bodily movement or posture in lifting the bottles and/ or hand movements for printing the labels onto the bottles;
ii. The Defendants had been on notice the task was causing the Claimant difficulties;.

iii. The Defendant increased the Claimant's targets to unrealistic levels which made the chance of causing injury more likely;
c. *Negligently and/or in breach of Regulation 4(1)(b) aforesaid, failed to take appropriate steps to reduce the risk of injury to the Claimant by providing suitable equipment to assist the Claimant;*
d. *Failed to undertake any or any adequate risk assessment;*
e. *Failed to have regard to:*
i. the physical suitability of the Claimant to carry out the operation;
ii. the results of any relevant risk assessment carried out pursuant to Regulation 3 of the Health Regulations;
iii. whether the Claimant was within a group of employees identified by that assessment as being especially at risk;
iv. the results of any health surveillance provided pursuant to Regulation 6 of the Health Regulations in breach of Regulation 4(3);
f. *Failed to make reasonable adjustments such as reducing the volumes of bottles the Claimant was required to deal with;*

2. Management of Health and Safety Regulations at Work 1999

a. *Failed to make a suitable and sufficient assessment of the risks to health and safety of the Claimant whilst at work in breach of Regulation 3(1)*
b. *Failed to review the assessment set out above, in breach of Regulation 3(3)*
c. *Failed to record the significant findings of the assessment and any group of its employees identified by it as being especially at risk in breach of Regulation 3(6)*
d. *Failed to:*
i. Avoid the risks and/or
ii. Evaluate the risks which could be avoided
iii. Combat the risks at source
iv. Replace the dangerous with non-dangerous or less-dangerous in breach of Regulation 4
e. *Failed to make and give effect to appropriate measures for the effective planning, organisation, control, monitoring and review of the preventative and protective measures in breach of Regulation 5(1)*
f. *Failed to record the measures set out at sub-paragraph (xiv) above in breach of Regulation 5(2)*

g. *Failed to ensure that the Claimant was provided with such health surveillance as appropriate in breach of Regulation 6*
h. *Failed to prove the Claimant with information as to:*
i. *The risks to his health and safety identified by the assessment*
j. *The preventative and protective measures to be taken in breach of Regulation 10(1).*

3. Workplace (Health, Safety & Welfare Regulations 1992):

a. *Negligently and/or in breach of statutory duty, in all the premises set out above, provided the Claimant with an unsafe place and system of work thereby exposing his to an unnecessary and unreasonable risk of injury*
b. *Failed to heed complaints made by the Claimant as set out above.*

4. Personal Protective Equipment at Work Regulations 1992

a. *Negligently and/or in breach of Regulation 4, failed to provide the Claimant with suitable personal protective equipment, such as aids or other PPE to reduce the risk of hand injuries*
b. *Negligently and/or in breach of Regulation 8, failed to make an assessment to determine whether any personal protective equipment they intended to provide would be suitable*
c. *Negligently and/or in breach of Regulation 5, failed to make an assessment of whether such equipment was compatible and continued to be effective against the risk or risks in question*
d. *In all the premises set out above, provided the Claimant with an unsafe place and system of work, thereby exposing him to an unnecessary and unreasonable risk of injury.*

WRULD – Repetitive Strain – Example Case

ANN WILSON v BAXTERSTOREY LTD (2012) - An employer was not liable for a de Quervains type repetitive strain injury caused to a chef's thumb, where the chef had adopted a work practice of holding mixing bowls using a pincer grip. The activities were undertaken for a very short time and for limited periods during the day and did not give rise to any foreseeable risk of injury or any requirement for a risk assessment. The Judgment said:-

> "*The Claimant's case was set out in a skeleton argument by Mr. Hiorns as follows:*
>
> *she mixed up to 10 salads each day in a large aluminium bowl. Each salad was then spooned out into a melamine dish. When doing this the Claimant held the bowl in her left hand using her thumb inside the bowl and making a pinch grip with the fingers of that hand. Each spooning process took 2 to 3 minutes. After each salad mix the Claimant cleaned the bowl at the sink, holding it with her left thumb as before for 1 minute or so.*
>
> *On 3 days each week the Claimant made cakes. She made sponge cake mix in a large stainless steel bowl in an electric mixer. This was scooped out into cake rings whilst she held the bowl with her left thumb as before. This took 8 to 10 minutes.*
>
> *She made rock cakes in the same bowl and spooning out this mix took 5 to 8 minutes. Flapjacks and date crispy crunch were made in saucepans and the mix was spooned out whilst the Claimant held the saucepan with her thumb on the inside of the saucepan, holding it at an angle. Flapjacks took 8 to 10 minutes to scoop out and the date crispy crunch took 6 to 8 minutes.*
>
> ***The Claimant's case is that her injury was caused by the additional workload required of her in the two weeks prior to going on holiday in June 2009. She was required to make sufficient extra sponge cakes, rock cakes, flapjacks and date crispy crunch to last in the restaurant whilst she was away. This additional work led to the Claimant developing a swelling on her left wrist and subsequently de Quervain"s stenosing tenovaginitis was diagnosed.***
>
> *The basis of the Claimant's case is that the Claimant's method of holding the salad bowls, cake mix bowls and saucepan using a pincer grip with her left thumb was unsafe.*

Under the Management of Health and Safety at Work Regulations 1999 a risk assessment should have been undertaken.

More specifically, as the tasks in question were manual handling operations for the purposes of the ***Manual Handling Operations Regulations 1992, a risk assessment should have been made in respect of these operations - Regulation 4(1)(b)(i).***

For there to be a duty to undertake such a risk assessment all that is required is that there is a foreseeable possibility of injury - O'Neill v DSG Retail Ltd [2002] EWCA Civ 1139.

The risk assessment is a vital tool as it "should be a blueprint for action" - Allison v London Underground Ltd [2008] EWCA Civ 71.

In the present case no risk assessment was made in respect of the Claimant's manhandling of the salad bowls, cake mix bowls or saucepans.

The Defendants undertook a number of risk assessments in respect of equipment in the kitchen - pages 502-552. One relates to manual handling (page 544) but it is a generic assessment and considers no specific tasks.

The Claimant's case is that a risk assessment was required as there was a foreseeable possibility of injury of some kind from the manual handling operation which involved:
(i) bearing the load of the bowls and saucepans;
(ii) using only one hand;
(iii) holding them by the rim;
(iv) using a pinch grip;
(v) for a length of time.

Schedule 1 to the Manual Handling Operations Regulations 1992 directs an employer to have regard to the load in question and whether it is heavy or difficult to grasp. If these matters had been considered by the Defendants they ought to have appreciated that the bowls manhandled by the Claimant were - when full - comparatively heavy and difficult to grasp by the rim in one hand using a pinch grip involving the thumb.

The Health & Safety Executive's guidance notes to the Manual Handling Operations Regulations 1992 stress (at paragraph 39) the importance of involving employees in the assessment process. They also expand on the requirement to consider whether the load is difficult to grasp (at paragraph 83).

If the Claimant had been involved in an assessment of the tasks in question and she had been observed holding the bowls and saucepan then the assessment would have revealed that the way she held them was unsafe.

***Steps should then have been taken to comply with Regulation 4(1)(b)(ii) of the Manual Handling Operations Regulations 1992 which requires the risk of injury to be reduced to the lowest level reasonably practicable.** The obvious steps would have been to provide a warning to the Claimant about the risk involved with using such a pinch grip and to provide appropriate instruction and/or training in a safe method of transferring the contents of the bowls and saucepan as necessary.*

Even without a formal risk assessment, the Defendants should have been aware that the Claimant had adopted this unsafe habit. With such knowledge, they were under a duty to take steps to correct the habit by appropriate warning, instruction and/or training. Cases worthy of note include: McSherry v British Telecommunications plc [1992] 3 Med LR 129, Conaty v Barclays Bank plc (6 April 2000, Fifield v Denton Hall Legal Services [2006] EWCA Civ 169, Allison v London Underground Limited [2008] EWCA Civ 71.
By failing to correct the Claimant's use of her left thumb in an unsafe manner the Defendants were in breach of the Manual Handling Operations Regulations 1992 and also in breach of their common law duty to devise and operate a safe system of work for the Claimant".

The Judge found:-

> "*Conclusion - I have no difficulty at all in concluding that this claim must fail on liability. I do not accept that the work practices as now identified caused the injury and I consider that, on the evidence that I have heard the DQT is likely to have been idiopathic. I accept Mr.Giddins' evidence that DQT may be idiopathic.* ***I also accept his evidence that her work practices, as identified in this judgment, are an unlikely cause of her DQT.***
>
> *Those are my primary findings on the issue of causation.* ***However, I also wish to record further that I find that Mr.s. Wilson has been such an unreliable historian that it is not possible to view her evidence as giving a reliable account of the experiences of her wrist and thumb.*** *It is not for the defendant to unearth or speculate about other potential causes for her condition or the reasons why her condition became more painful in June 2009.*
>
> *137.I realise that it is unusual to begin conclusions by referring to causation first (i.e. before the issue of breach of duty). However I have done so because part of the analysis of breach is that it is suggested that the causation of Mr.s. Wilson's DQT at work shows that there was a foreseeable possibility of injury arising from her system of work. I reject that suggestion.*
>
> *138.Having, I hope, expressed in full my conclusions on the facts behind Mr.s. Wilson's claim.* ***I reject the contention that they raised any foreseeable possibility of injury. I accept Ms Foster's submission (save as struck through by me and supplemented by the words in square brackets) that (a) these activities were not unduly onerous, whether a pinch grip was used or not; (b) were only undertaken for a matter of seconds at a [very short time] and only for limited periods of time during the day; (c) were not repetitive or forceful; and (d) did not accordingly give rise to the alleged or any foreseeable risk of injury". That being so, I did not accept that there was a need for a risk assessment of how Mr.s. Wilson should have emptied the contents of the mixing bowls. I consider that to be such a mundane task involving no foreseeable***

possibility of injury that the requirement for an assessment did not arise.

139.If the employees had been involved in any discussions about these work practices I do not think that there can be any sensible suggestion that such discussions would have demonstrated the need to change the way that bowls were emptied by Mr.s. Wilson. She did not see any problem with it over the course of her employment and I have no evidence to suggest that there have been any other complaints about it either. Therefore I do not consider that the Health and Safety Executive guidance notes at page 24 of Mr. Hiorns' bundle assist the claimant at all on the facts of this case.

*140.**As to the common law duty I do not consider that there was anything unsafe about the system of work. I do not see how it can possibly be said to be unsafe for an employee to decant this limited number of bowls in the manner that I have described over this limited amount of time".***

WRULD Quantum

There are many examples of work related upper limb disorders. Please refer to the relevant section of the 14th edition of the Judicial College Guidelines.

WULRD Key Points

1. The Manual Handling Regulations and the PUWER Regulations will be important.

2. The key is to look at the risk assessment and how any potential exposure to RSI has been reduced to the lowest level if it cannot be eliminated.

3. You must ensure that the activity complained of is likely to cause an RSI related condition such as Carpal Tunnel Syndrome and

that the link between the activity and the injury is explained by the expert.

4. The medical evidence must also explain the specific condition complained of and how it can be caused.

5. If the Defendant has carried out a specific adequate risk assessment and implemented it- the case may be problematic on prospects.

CHAPTER TEN

ASBESTOS AND MESOTHELIOMA RELATED CLAIMS – BREACH OF DUTY, CAUSATION AND QUANTUM

Asbestos related litigation cases tend to be of significant value and are extremely complicated. Indeed, the same could likely attract a whole book on their own. However, the aim of this short chapter is to provide an overview of these conditions, breach of duty and quantum, considering the basic principles as opposed to in depth analysis.

As referred to above, it is absolutely essential for any practitioner intending to litigate such claims to read and have a very good understanding of ***Fairchild v Glenhaven Funeral Services Ltd*** [2002] UKHL 22 for asbestos cases as applied to lung cancer cases in *Carl Heneghan (Son & Executor of James Leo Heneghan, Deceased) v Manchester Dry Docks Ltd & Ors* [2016] EWCA Civ 86. These cases show how the usual balance of probabilities test in causation has had to be modified to incorporate a test of increased risk due to the nature of causation in such cases being impossible to establish on normal principles.

Fairchild v Glenhaven **[2002] 3 WLR 89** House of Lords was a conjoined appeal involving three claimants who contracted mesothelioma, a form of lung cancer contracted by exposure to asbestos. The condition does not get worse the greater the exposure. Once the fibre has embedded into the lung it can lay dormant for 30-40 years before giving rise to a tumour which can then take 10 years to kill. It will be only the last 1-2 years where a person may experience symptoms. By this time it is too late to treat. Each of the claimants had been exposed to asbestos by a number of different employers. They were unable to demonstrate, and medical science was unable to detect, which employer exposed each of them to the one fatal fibre. It was held if the claimants could demonstrate that one employer had materially increased the risk of contracting mesothelioma they were entitled to claim full compensation from that one employer.

There are various types of asbestos-related disease, pleural plaques, pleural fibrosis (thickening), asbestosis, lung cancer and mesothelioma. The definitions of each are set out below from the NHS website:- https://www.nhs.uk/conditions/asbestosis/

Asbestosis is a serious long-term lung condition caused by prolonged exposure to asbestos.

Asbestos is a whitish material that was used in buildings for insulation, flooring and roofing in the past, but is now no longer used. While asbestos can be dangerous, it doesn't present a health risk if left undisturbed. But if material containing asbestos is damaged, it can release a fine dust that contains asbestos fibres. When the dust is breathed in, the asbestos fibres enter the lungs and can gradually damage them over time. But you would need prolonged exposure to asbestos fibres, usually over many years, before you develop asbestosis.

Am I at risk?

You may have been exposed to asbestos if you worked in an industry such as building or construction, particularly in the 1970s-90s. Now that asbestos is no longer used, those most at risk of being exposed to asbestos include people whose jobs put them at risk of damaging any asbestos remaining in old buildings, such as electricians and demolition workers. For more information on who could be at risk, read Health and Safety Executive (HSE): am I at risk?

Symptoms of asbestosis

Breathing in asbestos fibres over many years eventually causes scarring of the lungs. Symptoms of this can include:

- *shortness of breath*
- *persistent cough*
- *wheezing*
- *extreme tiredness (fatigue)*
- *pain in your chest or shoulder*
- *in more advanced cases, clubbed (swollen) fingertips*

Complications of asbestosis

People with asbestosis also have a higher risk of developing other serious conditions, such as:

- pleural disease – thickening of the lining covering the lungs (pleura)
- mesothelioma – cancer that affects the lining of the lungs, tummy, heart or testicles
- lung cancer

Breach of Duty

There are numerous regulations that are likely to be relevant but the main ones are as follows:-

1. Control of Asbestos at Work Regulations 2002.
2. Control of Asbestos at Work Regulations 1987.
3. Asbestos Regulations 1969.
4. Sections 29 (1) , 41 (1) and 63 of the Factories Act 1961.
5. Sections 4 (1) and 47 (1) of the Factories Act 1937.
6. Asbestos Industry Regulations 1931.

Mesothelioma Cases

The Compensation Act 2006 sets out:-

3 Mesothelioma: damages

(1) This section applies where—
(a) a person ("the responsible person") has negligently or in breach of statutory duty caused or permitted another person ("the victim") to be exposed to asbestos,

(b) the victim has contracted mesothelioma as a result of exposure to asbestos,
(c) because of the nature of mesothelioma and the state of medical science, it is not possible to determine with certainty whether it was the exposure mentioned in paragraph (a) or another exposure which caused the victim to become ill, and
(d) the responsible person is liable in tort, by virtue of the exposure mentioned in paragraph (a), in connection with damage caused to the victim by the disease (whether by reason of having materially increased a risk or for any other reason).

(2) The responsible person shall be liable—
(a) in respect of the whole of the damage caused to the victim by the disease (irrespective of whether the victim was also exposed to asbestos—
(i) other than by the responsible person, whether or not in circumstances in which another person has liability in tort, or
(ii) by the responsible person in circumstances in which he has no liability in tort), and
(b) jointly and severally with any other responsible person.

(3) Subsection (2) does not prevent—
(a) one responsible person from claiming a contribution from another, or
(b) a finding of contributory negligence.

(4) In determining the extent of contributions of different responsible persons in accordance with subsection (3)(a), a court shall have regard to the relative lengths of the periods of exposure for which each was responsible; but this subsection shall not apply—
(a) if or to the extent that responsible persons agree to apportion responsibility amongst themselves on some other basis, or
(b) if or to the extent that the court thinks that another basis for determining contributions is more appropriate in the circumstances of a particular case.

(5) In subsection (1) the reference to causing or permitting a person to be exposed to asbestos includes a reference to failing to protect a person from exposure to asbestos.

(6) In the application of this section to Scotland—
(a) a reference to tort shall be taken as a reference to delict, and
(b) a reference to a court shall be taken to include a reference to a jury.

(7) The Treasury may make regulations about the provision of compensation to a responsible person where—
(a) he claims, or would claim, a contribution from another responsible person in accordance with subsection (3)(a), but
(b) he is unable or likely to be unable to obtain the contribution, because an insurer of the other responsible person is unable or likely to be unable to satisfy the claim for a contribution.

(8) The regulations may, in particular—
F1(a). . . . .
(b) replicate or apply (with or without modification) a transitional compensation provision;
(c) provide for a specified person to assess and pay compensation;
(d) provide for expenses incurred (including the payment of compensation) to be met out of levies collected in accordance with section 213(3)(b) of the Financial Services and Markets Act 2000 (c. 8) (the Financial Services Compensation Scheme);
(e) modify the effect of a transitional compensation provision;
(f) enable the [F2Financial Conduct Authority or the Prudential Regulation Authority] to amend the Financial Services Compensation Scheme;
(g) modify the Financial Services and Markets Act 2000 in its application to an amendment pursuant to paragraph (f);
(h) make, or require the making of, provision for the making of a claim by a responsible person for compensation whether or not he has already satisfied claims in tort against him;
(i) make, or require the making of, provision which has effect in relation to claims for contributions made on or after the date on which this Act is passed.

F3(9). . . . .

(10) In subsections (7) and (8)—
(a) a reference to a responsible person includes a reference to an insurer of a responsible person, and
(b) "transitional compensation provision" means a provision of an enactment which is made under the Financial Services and Markets Act 2000 and—
(i) preserves the effect of the Policyholders Protection Act 1975 (c. 75), or
(ii) applies the Financial Services Compensation Scheme in relation to matters arising before its establishment.

(11) Regulations under subsection (7)—
(a) may include consequential or incidental provision,
(b) may make provision which has effect generally or only in relation to specified cases or circumstances,
(c) may make different provision for different cases or circumstances,
(d) shall be made by statutory instrument, and
(e) may not be made unless a draft has been laid before and approved by resolution of each House of Parliament.

Relevant Papers Regarding Asbestosis

The following publications may be relevant to the defendant's knowledge of asbestos:-

a) the Annual Reports of the Chief Inspecting Officer of Factories from 1899 regularly referred to the injurious nature of asbestos dust and the need for exhaust ventilation and respirators to combat asbestos dust;

b) in 1930 the Merewether and Price "Report on the Effects of Asbestos Dust on the Lungs and Dust Suppression in the Asbestos Industry" demonstrated the link between chronic exposure to asbestos dust and the development of asbestosis and recognised that workers were likely to be exposed to dust containing asbestos in various industries including the insulation of boilers, pipes and engines;

c) the Annual Report of the Chief Inspecting Officer of Factories for 1929 concluded that asbestosis can lead to complete disablement and death;

d) the Workmen's Compensation (Silicosis and Asbestosis) Act 1930 added asbestosis to the list of compensatable occupational diseases;

e) the Annual Report of the Chief Inspecting Officer of Factories for 1930 warned that exposure to heavy concentrations of asbestos dust for comparatively short periods resulted in the appearance sooner or later of disabling asbestosis;

f) the Asbestos Industry Regulations 1931 were passed and came into force on March 1st 1932;

g) pleural plaques associated with asbestos were first described by Gloyne in 1933;

h) the Annual Report of the Chief Inspecting Officer of Factories for 1938 concluded that dust inhaled is physiologically undesirable and dust thought then to be harmless might be discovered in the future to be dangerous, and noted the relationship between asbestosis and lung cancer;

i) the Annual Report of the Chief Inspecting Officer of Factories for 1945 recognised that the use of asbestos either alone or as part of a mixture for the purpose of heat and sound insulation increased the number of workers exposed to risk of injury to health through asbestosis and called for action. The letter from the Chief Inspector of Factories entitled "Asbestos Insulation Aboard Ships" dated August 1945;

j) the Annual Report of the Chief Inspecting Officer of Factories for 1949 warned that in dealing with the dangers arising on the handling of asbestos the maintenance of dust control and adequate exhaust ventilation at all points where dust may be evolved, was of the utmost importance and it was necessary to watch for the new use of asbestos in some manufacturing or other processes and the need to prevent the inhalation of asbestos dust or fibre in them;

k) the Annual Report of the Chief Inspecting Officer of Factories for 1952 noted the introduction of types of respirators that protected the wearer against inhalation of dust;

l) the Annual Report of the Chief Inspecting Officer of Factories for 1956 specifically identified the removal of old heat insulation lagging as a serious health hazard to those engaged on it;

m) papers by Wagner in 1960 and Newhouse & Thompson in 1965 reported the clear association between exposure to asbestos and Mesothelioma;

n) the Annual Report of the Chief Inspecting Officer of Factories for 1966 stressed that the provision of suitable respiratory protection preferably by positive pressure airline type, was essential for all persons exposed to dust in the course of removal of asbestos based lagging and of the need to protect not only those carrying out the process but all persons who may be in the location at the same time, and asserted that the only safe course is to eliminate the escape of asbestos dust into the air altogether;

o) the Annual Report of the Chief Inspecting Officer of Factories for 1967 stressed the need to minimise the evolution of asbestos dust by wetting lagging during removal and the wearing of respiratory protection such as positive pressure respirators during lagging removal and to segregate areas in which asbestos is being removed by polythene sheeting;

p) the Asbestos Regulations 1969 were passed and came into force on May 14th, 1970.

q) the Control of Asbestos at Work Regulations 1987.

Example Allegations of Negligence / Breach of Duty

1. Failure to warn.

2. Failure to provide breaching apparatus.

3. Failure to provide extraction equipment.

4. Failure to provide respiratory equipment.

5. Failure to risk assess and/ or remove the asbestos.

6. Failure to obtain expert advice.

Various breaches of statutory duty and Regulations will be required, but one should defer to Counsel as the pleadings are complex and will likely need to include a Provisional Damages Claims.

Date of Knowledge

As with other disease claims, the date of knowledge will vary from industry to industry, however, the case of *Stokes v Guest* is useful. In this matter, an employee had been exposed at work over a long period to mineral oil which, on a daily basis, had saturated his clothing and come into contact with his skin. As a result of this, he developed cancer of the scrotum from which he eventually died. The factory had known of the risk of scrotal cancer, had failed to draw the workforce's attention to the risk and had failed to institute periodic medical examinations of workers exposed to the risk.

Held: The court set down the test of an employer's duty when knowledge of a risk was developing, the test being that of the reasonable and prudent employer, taking positive thought for the safety of his workers in the light of what he knows or ought to know.

The Court said:-

Swanwick J: 'the overall test is still the conduct of the reasonable and prudent employer, taking positive thought for the safety of his workers in the light of what he knows or ought to know; where there is a recognised and general practice which has been followed for a substantial period in similar circumstances without mishap, he is entitled to follow it, unless in the light of common sense or newer knowledge it is clearly bad; but, where there is developing knowledge, he must keep reasonably abreast of it and not be too slow to apply it; and where he has in fact greater than average knowledge of the risks, he may be thereby obliged to take more than the average or standard precautions. He must weigh up the risk in terms of the likelihood of injury occurring and the potential consequences if it does; and he must balance against this the probable effectiveness of the precautions that can be taken to meet it and the expense and inconvenience they involve. If he is found to have fallen below the standard to be properly expected of a reasonable and prudent employer in these respects, he is negligent.'

Quantum

Please refer to the relevant section of the 14th edition of the Judicial College Guidelines.

Asbestos Related Case – An Example in Point

In ***ALBERT VICTOR CARDER v (1) SECRETARY OF STATE FOR HEALTH (2) UNIVERSITY OF EXETER (2015)v*** where a defendant was responsible for 2.3 per cent of the claimant's total exposure to asbestos, it was liable in proportion for damages for his asbestosis, and could not escape liability on the basis of evidence that that particular exposure had made no discernible difference to his condition. The Court looked a number of important authorities:-

First, Holtby v Brigham & Cowan (Hull) Limited [2000] ICR 1086 is the classical exposition on the award of damages for what all accept to be the divisible disease of asbestosis. It is divisible in the sense that all asbestos exposure, to put it neutrally at the moment, may contribute to the risk of its development, the fact of its development, and degree of its development, in direct proportion to exposure as opposed to indivisible conditions like mesothelioma where there is no evidence of association between the dose and either the causation or the extent of the disease if it does develop.

19 In the first judgment, with which Mummery LJ and Clarke LJ (as he then was) agreed, save in the latter's case on a subordinate point irrelevant to this case, Stuart-Smith LJ said:

"23. But it is said by Mr. May that there is no evidence to support his conclusion or justify the deduction of 25%. I do not agree. Although it is only a question of nomenclature I think Mr. Goldstaub is right when he submits that it is not so much a question of apportionment between tortfeasors as one of proof of causation in respect of a quantifiable part of his disability by the claimant against the defendant, and further it was not so much a question of discounting the full liability figure, as counting the proportion attributable to the defendant. But this is somewhat semantic and does not affect the judge's approach and conclusion.

25. It might be said that the judge should have made the defendants liable only to 50%. If the other employers had been before the court, then subject to exposure which ought to be considered de minimis, I think this is what he would have done. As it is he erred on the side of generosity to the claimant. No one criticises him for that."

20 Thus, Mr. Kent submits that the issue is one of causation not apportionment, that the Claimant has the burden of proof, and that he fails to discharge it on the evidence in this case.

Secondly, next, he prays in aid the equally classical decision in Cartledge v E. Jopling & Sons Ltd [1963] AC 758. He relies on the speech of Lord Pearce, who said at page 779:

"It is a question of fact in each case whether a man has suffered material damage by any physical changes in his body. Evidence that

those changes are not felt by him, and may never be felt, tells in favour of the damage coming within the principle of de minimis non curat lex. On the other hand, evidence that in an unusual exertion, or at the onslaught of disease, he may suffer from his hidden impairment tells in favour of the damage being substantial. There is no legal principle lack of knowledge in the plaintiff must reduce the damage to nothing or make it minimal."

This, Mr. Kent submits, establishes that changes that are not felt, and may never be felt, tells in favour of the damage coming within the principle of de minimis non curat lex.

22 Thirdly, finally, he submits that he finds support for that approach in Johnston v Chemical & Insulating Co. Ltd. [2007] UKHL 39, because Lord Hoffman said in his speech at paragraph 7:

"Some causes of action arise without proof of damage. Trespass and breach of contract are examples. Proof of the trespass or breach of contract is enough to found a cause of action. If no actual damage is proved the claimant is entitled to nominal damages. But a claim in tort based on negligence is incomplete without proof of damage. Damage in this sense is an abstract concept of being worse off physically economically, so that compensation is an appropriate remedy. It does not mean simply a physical change which is consistent with making one better, as in the case of a successful operation, or with being neutral, having no perceptible effect upon one's health or capability."

CHAPTER ELEVEN
THE FUTURE OF DISEASE CASES AND LASPO PART 2

The background behind the new intermediate track was set out in the 2017 Jackson report, which can be found at https://www.judiciary.gov.uk/wp-content/uploads/2017/07/fixed-recoverable-costs-supplemental-report-online-2-1.pdf. It sets out as follows:-

> ***1 Should there be any fixed recoverable costs above the fast track?***
>
> *1.1 The debate about fixed recoverable costs above the fast track. There has been much debate about whether there is any scope for introducing a fixed costs regime above the fast track. A large part of the legal profession is opposed to any extension of fixed costs above the current limit of £25,000. They put forward two principal arguments:*
> *(i) Multi-track cases are so varied in character that they do not lend themselves to any rigid costs matrix.*
> *(ii) Costs management is now working well in the multi-track (as noted in the preceding chapter). Therefore, there is no need for fixed costs.*
>
> *1.2 Conclusion. I acknowledge the force of both these arguments. In particular, I accept that recent improvements in costs management reduce the need for fixed costs. Nevertheless, after considering the extensive written submissions and the debates at the seminars,* ***I have concluded that there is scope for fixing the recoverable costs of some categories of cases above the fast track.***
>
> ***1.3 Recent evidence shows that the cost of litigating lower value cases in the multi-track remains disproportionate to the value of such cases. Applying a fixed recoverable costs ("FRC") regime to suitable cases will reduce the overall costs of litigation, by encouraging efficient working, together with streamlining and limiting the amount of work that needs to be done.*** *It will also eliminate the process costs of budgeting or assessing the costs of such cases on an*

individual basis. Furthermore, fixing recoverable costs creates a clear, transparent and predictable costs structure, which will enable parties to take an informed decision at the outset as to whether a proposed claim is worth pursuing or defending. This will be particularly valuable for litigants of modest means, including small and medium-sized enterprises. As the Birmingham Law Society observed in their submissions:

"Birmingham Law Society accepts that fixed fees can, in certain circumstances, bring certainty to parties considering and engaging in litigation. They can also offer transparency to members of the public looking to engage in litigation. As such Birmingham Law Society does not oppose the concept of fixed fees provided they are applied in the right circumstances/cases."

In my view it is now right to extend FRC above the fast track, but we must proceed with caution in order to protect access to justice.

1.4 How far above the fast track limit of £25,000 should any new FRC regime go? The Law Society, the Bar Council and others have argued that reform should be progressive and gradual, rather than a great leap forward. I accept that point. ***I also accept that we should not suddenly move to a universal FRC regime for all cases up to £250,000.1 I propose that there should be an upper limit of £100,000 and that only cases of modest complexity should fall within the new FRC regime.***

1.5 What sort of cases should go into the new FRC regime? The new FRC regime should apply to claims which are principally for monetary relief, such as damages or debt. The regime will include cases where declarations are sought largely to support claims for monetary relief. It will not be possible to evade the regime by including incidental claims for declaratory relief. In exceptional circumstances a claim for non-monetary relief may be assigned to the new FRC regime, where that is necessary to promote access to justice. For example:
(i) If individual householders are claiming an injunction to restrain private nuisance caused by a nearby industrial enterprise, they may

not be able to proceed unless their adverse costs risk is limited by an FRC regime.
(ii) Individuals of modest means bringing defamation claims because of material on the Internet (a growing category of claimants) may only feel comfortable proceeding if their adverse costs risk is limited by an FRC regime.

2 How should such a regime be structured?

2.1 Into what track should the new fixed costs cases go? There are three views about how we should provide for the new raft of fixed costs cases. First, these cases could remain in the multi-track but be subject to an FRC regime instead of costs management. Secondly, we could simply expand the fast track. The third option is to create a new track, sitting between the fast track and the multi-track, to provide for such cases. After full discussion at an assessors' meeting, the first option was rejected as impracticable. FRC cases will require a different case management regime and they will not be subject to costs management. You cannot have two entirely different streams of cases in the same track. So, the choice really lies between the second and third options.

2.2 I favour the third option for three reasons:
(i) The fast track works well. Practitioners are familiar with it. I do not want to change the character of a track which works well and already caters for a large proportion of all contested cases.
(ii) Cases in the bracket £25,000 to £100,000 will usually be more complex than fast track cases. They may require more elaborate evidence and take longer to try. The procedural rules for such cases should therefore be different from those in CPR Part 28.
(iii) The fast track upper limit of £25,000 coincides with the planned upper limit of the Online Solutions Court. When that court comes into existence it will replace the fast track as the normal court for many categories of claims up to

In chapter 9 below, however, I propose a separate capped costs regime for certain mercantile, chancery and TCC cases up to £250,000.

£25,000: see paragraphs 6.92-6.102 of Briggs LJ's Final Report.2 ***My proposed track will sit immediately above (a) the Online Solutions Court and (b) the residue of the fast track.*** *Joined up law reform requires that the different civil justice initiatives should dovetail together, as the former President of the Law Society emphasised in his speech at the London seminar.*

2.3 What should the new track be called? I propose that the new track be called the 'intermediate track'.

3 Allocation of cases to the intermediate track

3.1 Value cannot be the sole criterion. Many of the submissions make two important points. First, value must not be the sole criterion for assigning cases to an FRC regime: some high value cases are straightforward; some low value cases are complex; some cases are difficult to value. Secondly, if the recoverable costs are going to be fixed, the procedure must be streamlined, so that lawyers on both sides do less work. It follows from this second point that only cases suitable for a streamlined procedure should be allocated to the intermediate track.

3.2 Proposed criteria. I propose that the following be the criteria for allocating a case to the intermediate track:
(i) The case is not suitable for the small claims track or the fast track.
(ii) The claim is for debt, damages or other monetary relief, no higher than £100,000.
(iii) If the case is managed proportionately, the trial will not last longer than three days.
(iv) There will be no more than two expert witnesses giving oral evidence for each party.
(v) The case can be justly and proportionately managed under the expedited procedure described in section 4 below.
(vi) There are no wider factors, such as reputation or public importance, which make the case inappropriate for the intermediate track.
(vii) The claim is not for mesothelioma4 or other asbestos related lung diseases.

(viii) Alternatively, even if none of criteria (i)-(vii)are met, there are particular reasons to assign the case to the intermediate track, of the kind described in paragraphs 3.7-3.8 below.

3.3 Why exclude mesothelioma and other asbestos related lung diseases? These claims are managed in accordance with the procedure in the Mesothelioma Practice Direction (Practice Direction 3D). They are case managed in specific courts in specialist Asbestos Lists by judges experienced in this work. The law applying to the determination of such claims is in accordance with other personal injury claims, but in addition specific statutes and case law apply. The value of such claims varies. A few are of a value and/or level of complexity that would otherwise come within the intermediate track, principally claims for diffuse

3 The value of the case may change during the litigation for a variety of reasons. In the ordinary way, cases should remain within the track and band to which they were originally assigned. But if the case changes fundamentally, for example because the defendant admits part of the claim, then the court should have power to re-allocate.

4 There is a bespoke procedure for mesothelioma claims in Practice Direction 3D. Pleural thickening (many of which include a claim for provisional damages). Even so, I think that they should be excluded from the FRC regime. There is not always a clear distinction between mesothelioma cases and pleural thickening cases because (i) quite frequently the diagnosis is not clear-cut, at least in the early stages, and (ii) some claimants with relatively benign conditions will go on to develop mesothelioma or lung cancer or disabling respiratory disease. The Asbestos Lists are well used, operate very efficiently and have been the subject of few complaints from either claimants or defendant insurers. It would inevitably cause inefficiencies if some of these claims were removed from the specialist management provided by Practice Direction 3D, and case managed differently from other mesothelioma claims. That would defeat the aim of the Practice Direction.

3.4 What about complex personal injury claims and professional negligence claims? The criteria in paragraph 3.2 will exclude those complex personal injury and professional negligence cases which the Personal Injuries Bar Association and the Professional Negligence Bar Association maintain are unsuitable for FRC. My hope and expectation is that the criteria in paragraph 3.2 will catch only those cases which are suitable for FRC.

3.5 What about clinical negligence cases? As discussed in chapter 8 below, there is reason to believe that a bespoke process for clinical negligence claims up to £25,000 (including claims where breach and causation are in issue) with an accompanying grid of FRC, will result from the work which is in hand. Clinical negligence claims above £25,000 will seldom be suitable for the intermediate track, unless both breach of duty and causation have been admitted at an early stage. The multi-track will be the normal track for clinical negligence claims above £25,000.

3.6 Will some other categories of case generally be unsuitable for the intermediate track? Yes. On the basis of the above criteria, the intermediate track will seldom be suitable for (a) some multi-party cases; (b) actions against the police5 (as demonstrated by the submissions of the Police Action Lawyers Group); (c) child sexual abuse claims (as demonstrated by the submissions of the Association of Child Abuse Lawyers); and (d) intellectual property cases.

3.7 Additional discretion. The court should have a residual discretion to allocate any case not satisfying the criteria set out in paragraph 3.2 above (including any claim for non- monetary relief) to the intermediate track, where such allocation is necessary in order to promote access to justice. Paragraph 1.5 above gives examples of cases where such an order may be necessary to promote access to justice.

3.8 Cases where for other reasons recoverable costs should be limited. In some categories of litigation, where emotions are apt to run high, parties may need to be protected from their own enthusiasm for the fray.6 If mediation is unsuccessful or unacceptable to such parties, the straitjacket of the intermediate track may save them from ruinous litigation. This would be a factor to bear in mind on allocation.

3.9 The bands. ***Band 1 will be for the least complex cases in the intermediate track. A simple claim over the fast track limit, where there is only one issue and the trial will take a day or less, would generally be suitable for that band: for example, many debt claims or quantum only personal injury claims would be suitable for Band 1. Band 4 will be for the most complex cases in the intermediate track: Examples may be disputes about family businesses or boundary disputes between neighbours, where the disputed land has no great value. employers' liability disease claim where there are serious issues of fact/law and the trial is likely to last three days. Bands 2 and 3 will be the 'normal' bands for intermediate track cases, with the more straightforward cases going into Band 2 and the more complex cases going into Band 3.***

3.10 Pre-action process. ***The pre-action protocols should be amended to require the parties to endeavour to agree pre-action (a) the appropriate track for cases and (b) in respect of intermediate track cases, the appropriate band. Claimants should state their proposals in this regard in the letter of claim. Defendants should do the same in the letter of response.*** *If the case settles before issue or before allocation without any agreement on the appropriate track and band, then a decision on that issue should fall to the judge assessing costs.*

3.11 Assignment to bands at the allocation stage. ***On allocating a case to the intermediate track, the judge will (either by agreement between the parties or by reference to the directions questionnaires) assign it to Band 1, Band 2, Band 3 or Band 4. On issue, the claimant will have ascribed a value to their claim for court fee purposes.*** *That may assist the judge in the task of allocating cases to tracks and bands. At the subsequent case management conference ("CMC"), either party may challenge the assigned band. If the only reason for holding a CMC is the dispute about assignment, the unsuccessful party on that issue should incur a costs liability of £300 to the successful party.*

3.12 Need for a practice direction. ***There will need to be a practice direction for the intermediate track. This practice direction will include specific guidance on assignment to bands.8 Matters which are obviously relevant are: complexity of the factual and legal issues, volume of evidence, remedy sought and value of claim. A new directions questionnaire must be designed to elicit the information which the court will need for this task.***

3.13 Exiting the intermediate track. The court must have a residual power to take cases out of the intermediate track. It may be necessary to do so if the nature of the case changes fundamentally. The discretion should be strictly limited. Otherwise litigants will not enjoy certainty as to costs, which is one of the principal benefits of the fixed costs regime. I propose that the court should only be permitted to take cases out of the intermediate track after the first CMC "in exceptional circumstances".

4 Procedure for cases in the intermediate track

4.1 Requirement for a streamlined procedure. As previously noted, many of the written submissions have stressed that if recoverable costs are to be fixed, then the work to be done by the parties or their lawyers must also be controlled. This is necessary to ensure that the litigation process is efficient, so that only those steps that "are genuinely required in order to take a case to a fair trial" are taken (submission of the City of London Law Society). The procedure I propose below is intended to achieve that objective. Obviously, any rules embodying such a procedure must contain the familiar proviso "unless the court otherwise orders". For further discussion of how these principles will apply to personal injury and non-personal injury cases, see paragraphs 5.9 to 5.11 below. In the same way that the current CPR rule 26.8 gives guidance on allocation to tracks.

4.2 Statements of case. ***Each statement of case shall be no longer than 10 pages and shall be served together with any core document which are not in the possession of other parties. It should not be possible,*** *however, to evade the intermediate track by deliber-*

ately drafting particulars of claim to exceed the specified length. The court at the CMC will simply order the claimant to re-draft the pleading more concisely and at its own expense.

4.3 CMC. At the CMC, the court will review and approve a list of issues, resolve any disputed document requests, consider alternative dispute resolution ("ADR"), give directions and fix a date for the trial and (if it is needed) the pre-trial review ("PTR"). ***The court will also identify the specific matters to which any oral evidence should be directed and will limit the number of factual witnesses in the exercise of its powers under CPR rule 32.2 (3).*** *Although trials up to three days in length fall within the parameters of the intermediate track, both the advocates and the judge should bear in mind that trial days are the most expensive stage of the litigation and involve the most inconvenience to parties and witnesses (although not to lawyers, for whom trials are normal work). Therefore, they should together design case management directions to keep the trial as short as possible, ideally no more than one day.*

4.4 Disclosure in non-personal injury cases. CPR rules 31.5 (3) to (8) shall not apply. Instead, each party shall disclose:
(i) The documents upon which it relies, in so far as not previously disclosed;
(ii) Any documents or classes of documents which the court specifically orders at the CMC. The parties will exchange document requests seven days before the CMC.

4.5 Disclosure in personal injury cases. In personal injury litigation, disclosure is not generally a driver of high costs. Therefore, my Final Report recommended that personal injury litigation should be exempted from the proposed new disclosure rules: see chapter 37 paragraph 3.14. That recommendation was accepted and CPR rule 31.5 (2) exempts personal injury litigation from the new disclosure rules introduced in April 2013. For essentially the same reasons, ***I would exempt personal injury litigation from the proposed disclosure rules in the intermediate track. Standard disclosure will be the normal order in personal injury cases.***

4.6 Factual evidence. Written witness statements shall stand as evidence-in-chief. The total length of all the witness statements of a party shall not exceed 30 pages.

4.7 Expert evidence. Oral expert evidence shall be limited to one or, if reasonably required and proportionate, two expert witnesses for each party. Each expert report shall be no more than 20 pages. *This limit does not apply to any necessary photographs, plans and academic or technical articles attached to the report. In appropriate cases opposing experts shall give their evidence concurrently, in accordance with section 11 of Practice Direction 35.*

4.8 Trial. Oral evidence at trial shall be directed to the specific matters identified by the court at the CMC or subsequently. The court will set time limits for oral evidence and submissions (so far as it is necessary to do so), in order to complete the trial within its allotted span. In order to avoid argument about font size, the limit could be specified as a certain number of words. The same comment applies to all the suggested page limits in this chapter. In this context "core documents" means (a) documents relied upon by the party and (b) documents which are obviously necessary for other parties to understand the case they have to meet.

4.9 Applications. So far as possible, all applications should be made at the CMC. The rules for any applications made after the CMC should be:
(i) All applications and documents filed in support must be concise.
(ii) The respondent must answer in writing within 7 days of service of the application notice. The response must be concise.
(iii) Any reply from the applicant must be provided within two business days of
service of the response and be concise.
(iv) The court will deal with an application without a hearing unless the court
considers it necessary to hold a hearing. In appropriate cases that may be a hearing by telephone.

(v) The court will decide who shall pay the costs of any interim application and summarily assess them. Any such costs order will be additional to FRC.

4.10 Vexatious applications. The Bar Council make the point that the court must control "the scope and number of any interim applications or procedural gamesmanship". They give as examples repeated applications by a deep pocket party for specific disclosure or for answers to CPR Part 18 requests. I agree. The court should deal with such tactics by applying the rules governing unreasonable litigation conduct: see below.

4.11 Hand down of judgment. Whereas judges usually give ex tempore judgments in fast track cases, they will often wish to reserve judgment in intermediate track cases. This will necessitate a separate hand down hearing. It will be possible to dispense with the attendance of parties or advocates, if they have agreed all consequential matters. In the absence of such agreement, a short hearing is probably more efficient than continuing correspondence between the parties or their representatives.

5 Fixed recoverable costs

1.1 How should FRC be structured? This has been the subject of much debate, in particular at the Cardiff seminar. The Precedent H phases are suitable for costs management, but inevitably they generate argument about how much work in a particular phase has been done. Also, a party may do work earlier than is necessary for tactical reasons. In my view, the better approach for FRC is to draw up a grid by reference to chronological stages.11 This has worked in the fast track over the last four years and it brings greater certainty.

1.2 Ring fencing fees for counsel. Many practitioners, both solicitors and barristers, have urged the importance of ring fencing fees for counsel. The involvement of counsel at an early stage, both in advising and drafting, brings substantial benefits. Independent counsel bringing a fresh eye to the case can focus the litigation and sometimes bring about settlement. On the other hand, the rules cannot insist upon the use of counsel. Many other specialist lawyers bring the same benefits. In my view, for the reasons set out in chapter 5, the best course is to specify fees for items of work which are to be done by counsel or specialist lawyers.

5.3 Proposed grid. I propose a grid of FRC for intermediate track cases as set out in table 7.1 below. The grid must be read subject to the following rules:

11 As one of my assessors DJ Middleton and Stephen Webber (an experienced litigation solicitor) argued at the Cardiff seminar.
(i) In the grid the word 'damages' is used as shorthand for damages, debt, liquidated sum or other monetary relief.
(ii) If the claimant succeeds, the specified percentage applies to the sum recovered. If the defendant succeeds, the specified percentage applies to the claim defeated, as valued in the particulars of claim.
(iii) The figures in each of stages S1, S3, S4, S5, S6 and S8 are the cumulative totals for costs incurred up to and including that stage. I have shaded these cumulative boxes for ease of use.
(iv) The figures in stages S2, S7 and S9-S15 are separate sums for those items, if carried out.
(v) The figures in stages S2, S7 and S13 are ring-fenced for counsel or a specialist lawyer. The sums in the other boxes are for division between the solicitors and counsel/specialist lawyer as appropriate in the individual case.
(vi) For non-personal injury cases which are settled before issue, the figures in stage S1 are capped costs, rather than FRC.

Table 7.1

Stage (S)	***Band 1***	***Band 2***	***Band 3***	***Band 4***
S1 Pre-issue or pre-defence investigations	*£1,400 + 3% of damages*	*£4,350 + 6% of damages*	*£5,550 + 6% of damages*	*£8,000 + 8% of damages*
S2 Counsel/ specialist lawyer drafting statements of case and/or advising (if instructed)	*£1,750*	*£1,750*	*£2,000 12*	*£2,000 13*
S3 Up to and including CMC	*£3,500 + 10% of damages*	*£6,650 + 12% of damages*	*£7,850 + 12% of damages*	*£11,000 + 14% of damages*
S4 Up to the end of disclosure and inspection	*£4,000 + 12% of damages*	*£8,100 + 14% of damages*	*£9,300 + 14% of damages*	*£14,200 + 16% of damages*
S5 Up to service of witness statements and expert reports	*£4,500 + 12% of damages*	*£9,500 + 16% of damages*	*£10,700 + 16% of damages*	*£17,400 + 18% of damages*
S6 Up to PTR, alternatively 14 days before trial	*£5,100 + 15% of damages*	*£12,750 + 16% of damages*	*£13,950 + 16% of damages*	*£21,050 + 18% of damages*
S7 Counsel/ specialist lawyer advising in writing or in conference (if instructed)	*£1,250*	*£1,500*	*£2,000*	*£2,500*
S8 Up to trial14	*£5,700 + 15% of damages*	*£15,000 + 20% of damages*	*£16,200 + 20% of damages*	*£24,700 + 22% of damages*
S9 Attendance of solicitor15 at trial per day16	*£500*	*£750*	*£1,000*	*£1,250*

12 £3,000 if there is a counterclaim and defence to counterclaim. The rules may need to specify how costs are split between claim and counterclaim.

13 £3,000 if there is a counterclaim and defence to counterclaim. The rules may need to specify how costs are split between claim and counterclaim.

14 If the receiving party did not prepare the bundle, subtract: (a) £500 for a Band 1 case, (b) £750 for a Band 2 case, (c) £1,000 for a Band 3 case, and (d) £1,250 for a Band 4 case.

15 In this table "solicitor" includes a representative of the solicitor's firm

16 To be halved if attendance is for half a day or less.

Stage (S)	*Band 1*	*Band 2*	*Band 3*	*Band 4*
S10 Advocacy fee: day 1	*£2,750*	*£3,000*	*£3,500*	*£5,000*
s11 Advocacy fee: subsequent days17	*£1,250*	*£1,500*	*£1,750*	*£2,500*
S12 Hand down of judgment and consequential matters	*£500*	*£500*	*£500*	*£500*
S13 ADR: counsel/specialist lawyer at mediation or JSM (if instructed)	*£1,200*	*£1,500*	*£1,750*	*£2,000*
S14 ADR: solicitor at JSM or mediation	*£1,000*	*£1,000*	*£1,000*	*£1,000*
S15 Approval of settlement for child or protected party	*£1,000*	*£1,250*	*£1,500*	*£1,750*
Total: (a) £30,000 (b) £50,000, (c)	*(a) £19,150*	*(a) £33,250*	*(a) £39,450*	*(a) £53,050*

£100,000 damages18	*(b) £22,150 (c) £29,650*	*(b) £37,250 (c) £47,250*	*(b) £43,450 (c) £53,450*	*(b) £57,450 (c) £68,450*

1.3 Why should the figures in stage S1 be FRC in personal injury cases but capped costs in other cases? In personal injury cases, there is a minimum amount of work which must be done to achieve a settlement pre-issue. On a 'swings and roundabouts' basis the S1 figures can fairly stand as FRC in personal injury cases. In non-personal injury cases, the amount of work to be done to achieve a pre-issue settlement may vary substantially. In some cases, a simple letter of claim may suffice to bring about a settlement. In other cases, a large amount of investigation may be required.

1.4 How are the costs figures derived? The figures in Table 7.1 are based upon (a) Professor Fenn's analysis of data on personal injury cases received from Taylor Rose TTKW,19 (b) discussions with the assessors, (c) consideration of the budget exercise, the submissions and data received and (d) my view as to how CPR rule 44.3 (5) (defining proportionality) should be applied to cases falling within the intermediate track. By way of elaboration:

(i) The graphs at appendix 9 show all 1,461 observations extracted from the Taylor Rose TTKW dataset relating to multi-track claims settled since the coming into force of the Legal Aid, Sentencing and Punishment of Offenders Act 2012 with damages less than £100,000 and where the claimants had provided no more than three expert reports. Each separate chart in the graphs contains those observations on claims that were settled at four different chronological stages of litigation - pre-issue, pre-CMC, pre-expert exchange, pre-PTR. The dots show the observed combinations of agreed costs and damages at settlement for each claim, where agreed costs are measured on the vertical axis, and damages on the horizontal axis. Within each chart, several lines are drawn through the data. The lines labelled "Band 1" (i.e. the first from the bottom in each chart) show the expected agreed costs as estimated

17 To be halved if attendance is for half a day or less.

18 Assuming a one day trial in Band 1, a two day trial in Band 2, and a three day trial in Bands 3 and 4. For all bands, it is assumed that there was no counterclaim, that the receiving party prepared the trial bundles, that there was unsuccessful ADR and that there was no approval of settlement for a child or protected party.

19 Solicitors and costs lawyers. for varying levels of damages for the claims categorised as non-personal injury road traffic accident ("RTA"). The lines labelled "Band 2" (i.e. the second from the bottom in each chart) show the expected agreed costs as estimated for varying levels of damages for the claims categorised as RTA, employers' liability accident, or public liability. The lines labelled "Band 3" (i.e. the third from the bottom in each chart) show the expected agreed costs as estimated for varying levels of damages for the claims categorised as employers' liability disease. The lines labelled "Band 4" represent an attempt, by extrapolation and based on judgement, to characterise the relationship between agreed costs and damages for the most complex claims, irrespective of claim type. A formula is derived to produce each of these lines for the purposes of Table 7.1. The slope of each line is used to determine the '% of damages' figure attached to Bands 1 to 3. From inspecting the graphs, it is evident that as the complexity of the case (and the stage of litigation at settlement) increases the slope becomes steeper, and this leads to a higher '% of damages' figure. Based on the formula derived for each line, the lump sums are calculated as constant amounts of costs, irrespective of the level of damages. This is the point at which each line intersects the vertical axis. The Band 4 '% of damages' and lump sums are based on judgement for the most complex cases, using a similar relationship between agreed costs and damages to the other bands. Further explanation of how these formulae were estimated can be found in appendix 9.

(ii) I have then added to the fixed costs formulae the figures in the boxes for stages 2 and 7, in order to ring fence fees for counsel or specialist lawyers, as urged by many of those who sent in submissions or who spoke at seminars. In boxes S9 – S12 I have added in trial costs.

(Almost all of the cases analysed by Professor Fenn settled before trial and so did not include these costs.) Next, I have added in ADR costs. In personal injury cases below £100,000, this usually means direct negotiations or a joint settlement meeting. In non-personal injury cases below £100,000, ADR may involve a mediation. Finally, box S15 provides for settlements which may require court approval. That is discussed further in paragraph 6.2 below.

(iii) The figures in table 7.1 are broadly in line with the data set out in chapter 3 above (as discussed in paragraph 5.7 below) and with the experience of those assessors involved in the budgeting of cases suitable for the intermediate track.20 The figures in Bands 2 and 3 are reasonably close, because (a) that is where Professor Fenn's analysis of the Taylor Rose data leads and (b) most cases in this range tend to gravitate towards the centre. Bands 1 and 4 are for those cases which are simpler or more complex respectively.

5.6 Are you being more 'generous' than a strict derivation from the Fenn graphs? Yes. First, all the costs for stages S2, S7 and S9-S15 are all additional to the costs derived from the Fenn graphs. Secondly, the Band 4 figures go above that which can be derived statistically from the data, but fit with my own and my assessors' understanding of what are reasonable costs for the most complex types of case likely to go into the intermediate track.

20 Allowance must be made for process savings (because of FRC) and efficiency savings (because of the streamlined procedure for the intermediate track).

5.7 How do the figures in Table 7.1 compare with the data in chapter 3? In my view, there is a reasonable fit with the data in sections 2 and 4 of chapter 3, if one bears in mind the following:
(i) There will be 'process' savings, if recoverable costs are fixed.
(ii) There will be 'efficiency' savings consequent upon the streamlined procedure proposed in this chapter.
(iii) Approved budgets and many of the costs figures quoted in chapter 3 include disbursements which are additional to the sums shown in Table 7.1.

(iv) Not all of the cases up to £100,000 in value will go into the new intermediate track – only those which meet the criteria set out in this chapter. Many of the multi-track cases reviewed in chapter 3 self-evidently do not meet those criteria.

5.8 For the above exercise, I have ignored data received concerning cases which are unlikely to go into the intermediate track, such as substantial defamation claims and actions against the police. The damages in such cases may not be high, but their complexity indicates that they will not generally be suitable for the intermediate track.

5.9 How will the four-column grid be used in personal injury cases? Straightforward cases, where only one issue (such as quantum) is in dispute, will generally go into Band 1. Cases where both liability and quantum are in dispute will generally go into Band 2 or Band 3. Cases where there are serious issues on breach, causation and quantum (but which still fall within the intermediate track) will go into Band 4.

5.10 What about non-personal injury cases? Straightforward cases, where only one issue is in dispute (e.g. proving a debt), will generally go into Band 1. Most intermediate track cases will go into Band 2 or Band 3. Complex cases falling within the intermediate track will go into Band 4. The recoverable costs set out in Table 7.1 represent my best effort at converting the proportionality rules into hard figures. This must be the correct approach.21 The grid cannot be an exact pre-estimate of the costs which every party will incur in every intermediate track case. We do not have, and we never will have, large volumes of evidence about the costs of different types of non-personal injury cases comparable to the material available on personal injury claims. As the Chancery Bar Association observed in their paper on fixed costs last year:

"Traditionally litigants have had to expect to pay a substantial shortfall in the event of success where they are awarded costs on a standard basis."

5.11 Comparability of personal injury and non-personal injury cases. There is, I suggest, sufficient flexibility in the grid to accommodate the general run of personal injury and non- personal injury cases which fall within the intermediate track. Also, as one of my assessors has pointed out, within the intermediate track we should not be putting a higher price on property and financial claims than on claims about human health.

5.12 Disbursements. The above table does not include disbursements. The principal disbursements will be court fees, expert fees and (where ADR takes the form of mediation) the mediator's fee. In some cases, translators and/or interpreters are needed. I recommend that once the new fixed costs regime is in place, work should commence on developing fixed costs for experts. This is essentially what happened in the fast track. Once the fast track fixed costs for personal injury cases had been in place for a year, a scheme of fixed costs for medical reports22 was introduced: see chapter 15, paragraph 5.22 of my previous report and CPR rule 45.19. It would also be sensible to develop fixed costs for mediators, translators and interpreters.

5.13 ***Defendant's failure to beat claimant's Part 36 offer. If the defendant fails to beat an effective claimant offer under CPR Part 36, for the reasons set out in chapter 5 above and subject to the same caveats, I tentatively propose that there should be a 30% or 40% uplift on costs rather than indemnity costs.***

5.14 Unreasonable litigation conduct. In cases of unreasonable litigation conduct,23 the court should have the power either to award a percentage uplift on costs or to make an order for indemnity costs. The court will exercise that power, having regard to the seriousness of the conduct in question. One example of such unreasonable conduct might be substantial non-compliance with the relevant pre-action protocol.

5.15 London weighting. The current FRC rules in the fast track provide for a 12.5% uplift on fixed costs payable to a party who lives in the London area and instructs a legal representative who practises in the London area: see CPR rule 45.29C (2), rule 45.29F (5) and

Practice Direction 45 paragraph 2.6. I recommend that similar rules should apply to the extended FRC regime proposed in this chapter.

5.16 Uprating for inflation. I recommend that FRC in the intermediate track should be adjusted for inflation every three years, in the same manner as set out in chapter 5 concerning FRC in the fast track.

5.17 Contractual entitlement to costs. Any intermediate track case where one party has a contractual entitlement to costs will be subject to the streamlined procedure set out in this chapter. If the party with a contractual entitlement to costs is successful, the position will be as set out in chapter 5, paragraph 3.7. It is not within my terms of reference to consider whether the substantive law in this area should be reformed and I do not address that question.

6 Should the intermediate track include Part 8 claims?

6.1 Not yet. Some financial claims which proceed under CPR Part 8 would be suitable for FRC, as was noted at the Leeds seminar. It would be possible to modify the grid in Table 7.1 to accommodate those claims. The assessors and I have discussed at some length whether to propose FRC for such claims in this report. In the end, we have all concluded that such a step would be premature. For the time being, the costs of such claims should, where appropriate, be controlled by costs management. It is first necessary to let the intermediate track and the proposed FRC for Part 7 claims bed in. Many of the submissions to the review call for a gradualist approach to developing FRC. In relation to this issue, I heed their call. Subject to the minor exceptions set out below, I recommend that the question of extending FRC to Part 8 claims should be deferred for future consideration.

6.2 Approval of settlements for children and protected parties. Table 7.1 includes FRC for the approval of settlements for children and protected parties. If the settlement is pre- 22 In respect of soft-tissue injury RTA claims, which represent a large proportion of fast track personal injury claims.

As to what constitutes unreasonable litigation conduct, see Dammermann v Lanyon Bowdler LLP [2017] EWCA Civ 269 at [30]-[32].

24 Either 30% or 40%, depending upon what is decided in relation to the preceding paragraph issue, the application for approval is made under CPR Part 8. If proceedings are on foot, the application for approval is made under CPR Part 23. In any intermediate track case, the FRC for that application should be the same, regardless whether it is made under Part 8 or Part 23.25

1.3 Costs only proceedings. Costs only proceedings are brought under CPR Part 8. The receiving party files short particulars of claim referring to the settlement agreement, the defendant files an acknowledgement of service and the court makes an order for assessment of costs. I recommend that the FRC for a claimant in such proceedings should be £300 and for a defendant in such proceedings26 £150.

1.4 And finally. It should be noted that Part 8 is already used, in modified fashion, for determining quantum in low value personal injury cases not settled within the Portal. These cases already have FRC. They are excluded from the general rule that Part 8 claims are allocated to the multi-track. These arrangements will continue and are unaffected by my proposals in this chapter. These figures are, of course, exclusive of court fees and VAT.

7 The future

7.1 Bedding in of these reforms and future review. If the above proposals are accepted, I recommend that after four years there be a review of these arrangements. If they are working satisfactorily, then the Civil Procedure Rule Committee ("the Rule Committee") may decide to expand the scope of the intermediate track to include:
(i) Monetary claims above £100,000;
(ii) Claims for non-monetary relief.

7.2 Such an approach would give the reforms time to bed in, as well as enabling the Rule Committee to address any issues that arise. As one major insurer put it in their submission:

"any revised approach to fixed costs should be, to a degree, evolutionary so as to ensure that they are fair; proportionate; facilitate access to justice; make efficient use of limited and valuable court time and resources and prevent unintended consequences".

7.3 Analogy with the fast track. Such an approach would also replicate our experience with the fast track. There have been FRC for part of the fast track since July 2013. It is now widely accepted that it is appropriate to expand the scope of that fixed recoverable costs regime.

7.4 Developing more bespoke processes. I refer in chapter 8 to work which is in hand to develop bespoke processes for clinical negligence claims. There is scope for more work of this nature in respect of other areas of high volume litigation. Claimant and defendant representatives have worked together to develop bespoke processes for handling low value RTA claims and noise induced hearing loss claims. They have also worked together constructively to develop the Serious Injury Guide. Both the Association of Personal Injury Lawyers and the liability insurers speak warmly of that collaboration in their submissions.

25 Court fees will, of course, be a recoverable disbursement. 26 The paying party may occasionally secure an order for costs: for example, if the costs only proceedings fail for some reason or if there is a relevant CPR Part 36 offer.

Liability insurers lament that there is a gap between the fast track cases on the one hand and serious injury cases on the other, where there has been no such co-operation. They state:

"The parties (on both sides) have not worked together to create a consumer-friendly way of resolving disputes above the fast track threshold." I see much force in that comment and recommend that the collaboration between claimant bodies and liability insurers should now extend to areas of litigation above the fast track (whether or not within the intermediate track). This would be to the benefit of claimants as well as liability insurers and the legal profession. A

regime of FRC can probably be developed on the back of any further bespoke processes.

8 Conclusion

8.1 Recommendations. I recommend that:
(i) A new intermediate track with a streamlined procedure should be created for cases above the fast track, which are of modest complexity and up to a value of £100,000.
(ii) There should be a grid of FRC for such cases, as set out in this chapter, and the figures should be reviewed every three years.
(iii) There should be FRC for (a) applications to approve settlements for children and protected parties and (b) costs only proceedings, in respect of intermediate track cases.
(iv) Save as set out in (iii), CPR Part 8 claims should be excluded from the proposed FRC regime.
(v) After these reforms have bedded in, consideration should be given to extending the scope of the intermediate track and the range of FRC.

Key Points:-

1. There will be no immediate move for all cases up to £250,000, and the upper limit will be £100,000.

2. The intermediate track will sit immediately above (a) the Online Solutions Court and (b) the residue of the fast track.

3. There will be a number of specified criteria for allocation to the track (see 3.2 above).

4. The Court will have the power to re-allocate to the track.

5. Clinical negligence claims above £25,000 will seldom be suitable for the intermediate track, unless both breach of duty and causation have been admitted at an early stage. The multi-track will be the normal track for clinical negligence claims above £25,000.

6. Band 1 will be for the least complex cases in the intermediate track. A simple claim over the fast track limit, where there is only one issue and the trial will take a day or less, would generally be suitable for that band: for example, many debt claims or quantum only personal injury claims would be suitable for Band 1. Band 4 will be for the most complex cases in the intermediate track: Examples may be disputes about family businesses or boundary disputes between neighbours, where the disputed land has no great value. **Employers' liability disease claim where there are serious issues of fact/law and the trial is likely to last three days.** Bands 2 and 3 will be the 'normal' bands for intermediate track cases, with the more straightforward cases going into Band 2 and the more complex cases going into Band 3.

7. Pre-action process. The pre-action protocols should be amended to require the parties to endeavour to agree pre-action: (a) the appropriate track for cases and (b) in respect of intermediate track cases, the appropriate band. Claimants should state their proposals in this regard in the letter of claim. Defendants should do the same in the letter of response.

8. Exempt personal injury litigation from the proposed disclosure rules in the intermediate track. Standard disclosure will be the normal order in personal injury cases.

9. How will the four-column grid be used in personal injury cases? Straightforward cases, where only one issue (such as quantum) is in dispute, will generally go into Band 1. Cases where both liability and quantum are in dispute will generally go into Band 2 or Band 3. Cases where there are serious issues on breach, causation and quantum (but which still fall within the intermediate track) will go into Band 4.

10. A Defendant's failure to beat claimant's Part 36 offer -if the defendant fails to beat an effective claimant offer under CPR Part 36, for the reasons set out in chapter 5 above and subject to the same caveats, it tentatively proposes that there should be a 30% or 40% uplift on costs rather than indemnity costs.

11. Part 8 proceedings will not initially be included. There should be FRC for (a) applications to approve settlements for children and protected parties and (b) costs only proceedings, in respect of intermediate track cases.

12. The reforms once implemented will be reviewed in four years time.

MORE BOOKS BY LAW BRIEF PUBLISHING

'Occupiers, Highways and Defective Premises Claims: A Practical Guide Post-Jackson – 2nd Edition' by Andrew Mckie
'A Practical Guide to Financial Ombudsman Service Claims' by Adam Temple & Robert Scrivenor
'A Practical Guide to the Law of Enfranchisement and Lease Extension' by Paul Sams
'A Practical Guide to Marketing for Lawyers – 2nd Edition' by Catherine Bailey & Jennet Ingram
'A Practical Guide to Advising Schools on Employment Law' by Jonathan Holden
'Certificates of Lawful Use and Development: A Guide to Making and Determining Applications' by Bob Mc Geady & Meyric Lewis
'A Practical Guide to the Law of Dilapidations' by Mark Shelton
'A Practical Guide to the 2018 Jackson Personal Injury and Costs Reforms' by Andrew Mckie
'A Guide to Consent in Clinical Negligence Post-Montgomery' by Lauren Sutherland QC
'A Practical Guide to Running Housing Disrepair and Cavity Wall Claims: 2nd Edition' by Andrew Mckie & Ian Skeate
'A Practical Guide to the General Data Protection Regulation (GDPR)' by Keith Markham
'A Practical Guide to Digital and Social Media Law for Lawyers' by Sherree Westell
'A Practical Guide to Holiday Sickness Claims – 2nd Edition' by Andrew Mckie & Ian Skeate
'A Practical Guide to Inheritance Act Claims by Adult Children Post-Ilott v Blue Cross' by Sheila Hamilton Macdonald
'A Practical Guide to Elderly Law' by Justin Patten
'Arguments and Tactics for Personal Injury and Clinical Negligence Claims' by Dorian Williams
'A Practical Guide to QOCS and Fundamental Dishonesty' by James Bentley
'A Practical Guide to Drone Law' by Rufus Ballaster, Andrew Firman, Eleanor Clot
'Practical Mediation: A Guide for Mediators, Advocates, Advisers, Lawyers, and Students in Civil, Commercial, Business, Property, Workplace, and Employment Cases' by Jonathan Dingle with John Sephton

'Practical Horse Law: A Guide for Owners and Riders' by Brenda Gilligan

'A Comparative Guide to Standard Form Construction and Engineering Contracts' by Jon Close

'A Practical Guide to Compliance for Personal Injury Firms Working With Claims Management Companies' by Paul Bennett

'A Practical Guide to the Landlord and Tenant Act 1954: Commercial Tenancies' by Richard Hayes & David Sawtell

'A Practical Guide to Personal Injury Claims Involving Animals' by Jonathan Hand

'A Practical Guide to Psychiatric Claims in Personal Injury' by Liam Ryan

'Introduction to the Law of Community Care in England and Wales' by Alan Robinson

'A Practical Guide to Dog Law for Owners and Others' by Andrea Pitt

'Ellis and Kevan on Credit Hire – 5th Edition' by Aidan Ellis & Tim Kevan

'RTA Allegations of Fraud in a Post-Jackson Era: The Handbook – 2nd Edition' by Andrew Mckie

'RTA Personal Injury Claims: A Practical Guide Post-Jackson' by Andrew Mckie

'On Experts: CPR35 for Lawyers and Experts' by David Boyle

'An Introduction to Personal Injury Law' by David Boyle

'A Practical Guide to Claims Arising From Accidents Abroad and Travel Claims' by Andrew Mckie & Ian Skeate

'A Practical Guide to Cosmetic Surgery Claims' by Dr Victoria Handley

'A Practical Guide to Chronic Pain Claims' by Pankaj Madan

'A Practical Guide to Claims Arising from Fatal Accidents' by James Patience

'A Practical Approach to Clinical Negligence Post-Jackson' by Geoffrey Simpson-Scott

'A Practical Guide to Personal Injury Trusts' by Alan Robinson

'Employers' Liability Claims: A Practical Guide Post-Jackson' by Andrew Mckie

'A Practical Guide to Subtle Brain Injury Claims' by Pankaj Madan

'The Law of Driverless Cars: An Introduction' by Alex Glassbrook

'A Practical Guide to Costs in Personal Injury Cases' by Matthew Hoe

www.ingramcontent.com/pod-product-compliance
Lightning Source LLC
LaVergne TN
LVHW052312200926
848481LV00002B/536